LIMITED ENGAGEMENT

A Way of Living

Jacquelyn Shah

Winner of the 2022

Kenneth Johnston Nonfiction Book Award

Choeofpleirn Press
2023

Copyright, Jacquelyn Shah

2023

Choeofpleirn Press, LLC

All rights reserved.
This book may not be reproduced, in whole or in part,
including illustrations, in any form for any purposes other
than scholarly discussion or reviewing, without written
permission from the publishers.

Cover Art by Zarina Shah

ISBN: 979-8-9877852-3-2

Dedicated only to those humans
who are committed to peaceful living.

Insignificance is all we have.
	--John Ashbery, "Heavenly Days"

The fact that life has no meaning is a reason to live—
moreover, the only one.
	–E. M. Cioran

Existence is no more than
the precarious attainment of relevance
in an intensely mobile flux of past, present, and future.
	–Susan Sontag,
	"Thinking Against Oneself: Reflections on Cioran"

To detach yourself elegantly from the world;
to give contour and grace to sadness;
a solitude in style; a walk that gives cadence to memories;
...the past reborn in the overflow of fragrances...

–E. M. Cioran, *The Book of Delusions*
published in *Hyperion: On the Future of Aesthetics,*
a web publication of *The Nietzsche Circle,*
Volume V, issue 1, May 2010

CONTENTS

Outsider	1
Home Again	22
Detached, Unraveling, Dismissed, and Aftermath	44
Determination	65
S-E-X	76
Desultory Time	78
India, 1968	92
Invasions, 1970	100
Striving	106
London	111
How to Live and Write	118
No One Can Be Exactly Like You	135
Out of Body, Out of Mind	143
About the Author	157
Judge's Comments	159

ACKNOWLEDGEMENTS

Thanks to the editors of these journals and presses for the listed publications:

National Association Against Sexual Assault: "One Good Arm" 1992

South Coast Poetry Journal: "Letter from K on a Drunken Raft" 1993

Lit Fest Press / Festival of Language: "Letter from K on a Drunken Raft" and "We Will Not Stop Them" included in my published poetry book, *What to Do with Red*

Persimmon Tree: "Mutant" (version of "No One Can Be Exactly Like You") 2022

OUTSIDER

I.
I sit down under the pine tree, gather pine cones. I pick clover, try to make chains. A few somersaults and I roll around in the cool grass, then get up and walk to the front yard where I sit down on the doorsteps, see some kids playing down the way, at the edge of the road, kids I can't play with. I'm never allowed to leave my yard.

Ambling down our front walk to the street, I feel the sun hot on my neck, heavy pigtails growing damp from sweating. In the gravel bed edging the street, running the width of our yard, I begin to poke around, on a quest for pretty stones with mica, quartz. I'll save my treasures in a trunk meant for doll clothes. The road heats up, its tar bubbling, and I poke it with a stick, trying not to get the black gluey stuff on my clothes.

During a drizzle after lunch, I wait on the breezeway for the rain to stop, making little designs with tiles–blue, pink, yellow, white, peach–left over from Uncle Eddy's contract jobs. We have no car, so he uses our garage to store his materials. I'm lucky, I think, to have a kind, handsome uncle who gives me these tiles. After the rain stops, I ride my trike up and down the driveway for awhile, until I'm bored. Then I wander to the back.

Swing, jump! Swing, jump! Down to the grass, down the slide to the grass. Then...I dangle on the trapeze bar, a circus performer. Sometimes I'm cowboy shooting my cap gun; sometimes a seamstress stitching skirts for little dolls.

This is the day, maybe, when I pull down my pants to pee in the grass, so I don't have to knock on my mother's door.

She catches me doing it–watching from the kitchen window, I suppose–and drags me into the house. *You should know better!* she hisses. And then...the dreaded hairbrush spanking.

It was my domain, lovely and lonely, the yard around our little Pine Road house–my parents' first–where I spent much of my time from 1947 to 1955. During the day, with my father away at work, I was the only obstacle to my mother's prized solitude, and she neatly removed it by removing me. Sent out to play, I was issued stern directives: stay clean, don't knock at the door, which was always locked. So she was alone, I was alone, all day. Literally an outsider, I rarely played in the house, though I ate breakfast at the kitchen table by a window, watching chipmunks scamper over our stone grill, itching to get outside. At lunchtime, I was served my sandwich and milk at a picnic table where I ate alone, my mother returning to the house.

Playing outside morning to evening all day, before I was old enough for school, I became intimate with the silent trees and bushes, flowers, and weeds. Hearing the names from my parents–wild cherry, yew, catalpa, spruce, maple, pine–I learned to associate them with the trees. Where in the yard everything flourished in summer, what things languished in winter, I still remember. Yews on either side of the front door steps, catalpas flanking the cement walk to the street, a small blue spruce on one side of the house, a young maple towards the other side, close to the street. A towering pine on the side of the house with the greater expanse of lawn ending in an ugly spread of weeds between our yard and the neighbor's. Spirea or *bridal lace*, a term enchanting to me as a child, spread across the far side of our detached garage, where, beneath its dense branches and blossoms, nestled along the edge of the wall, were lilies of the valley. Though they were hidden, I never forgot to go to them in spring to breathe their faint fragrance.

Across from the garage, along the side yard fence, were low-growing crabapples and a tall bush whose name I never learned, its berries like diminutive tomatoes. Playing chef, I'd tear the leaves like lettuce, adding the ersatz tomatoes, tossing a salad for my make-believe restaurant patrons, then serving crabapple mudpie for dessert. I'm happy not knowing the name of that one bush; there's a mystique, alluring, that surrounds the not-knowing of some small thing etched in the mind.

By the side porch were peonies, their slightly feathery petals pale pink, one bush the less common red. They always seemed to be host, though, to fat black ants, which seemed to love crawling onto my arms when I tried to pick a blossom. But certain bugs were intriguing—like the daddy longlegs, picking their way through cool, shady areas, and fuzzy caterpillars, which I'd try to pet like I would a cat. But I hated chiggers and mosquitos, was terrified of wasps and bees. My favorite was the lightning bug. Catching and dispatching many to jars each summer, I was fascinated by their belly-lights winking against the glass. Bagworms that infested our catalpas one year were interesting, but my mother railed against them.

"Shizen! Goddamn-to-hell those worms!" She'd carp, *shizen* being her favorite obscenity, which she said meant *shit* in German. I didn't understand why it was okay to say it in German, which she implied was less offensive than the English. None of the other women in our family cursed, but she had been influenced by my father, whose curses were many, if relatively mild by today's standards. *Fuck*, whose ubiquity now pretty much undermines its pungency, was never heard in our house.

Some flowers of the Queen Anne's lace, a spot of beauty in our side-yard weeds, had deep purple specks in the center and others did not; I wondered why. Behind those weeds was the forbidden woods, full of blackberry bushes and poison ivy, populated by snakes. Very occasionally one could be seen slithering through our yard, and once, when Aunt Helen, my mother's sister, had joined my parents in berry-picking for pies, she reached for a cluster of blackberries, touched a black snake instead. She quickly withdrew, shrieking as she ran out of the woods.

"Never again! I'm never picking blackberries here again!" she insisted.

Along the back fence wild cherry trees formed a barrier to the woods, their little deep-purple cherries tasty only to birds, who would peck the pulp and leave behind nut-like seeds trailing bits of fruit, which dried to black in the sun. I dared to play with this waste, cracking the nuts to see what was inside. Unpecked cherries were tempting, too, and I'd smush them with my fingers, lick the smear of juice, wipe my hands on my shorts.

You're filthy, my mother would chastise at the end of the day, taking me straight to the cellar to clean up before supper. She soaped, then rinsed me with a hose connected to the washtub faucet since bathing in the bathroom was prohibited. I was far too dirty to be in my mother's bathroom, whose sparkle and gleam was eternal.

During rain and severe winter weather, I was deported to the cellar, a slightly damp, creepy place, not without interest. Exposed pipes, workbench, clotheslines, furnace and coal bin, deep washtubs, a washer with a wringer, a cupboard with jellies and jams—the basement was where I practiced my roller skating, going round and round the poles, faster and faster and faster! It was where I perfected writing letters on a chalkboard my mother had added to the dark corner where my toys and games were kept. Though I had no one to play games with during the day, occasionally in the evening I'd pull out the Chinese checkers and my parents would sit down with me to play on the living room floor.

There were steps going up from cellar to kitchen and two-thirds of the way was a landing and door to the breezeway that connected our house to the garage. Once I sat there writing what I thought would be a book about kids who had discovered, beyond their back yard, land surrounded by water and shaped like an Indian's head. *Mystery at Indian Head Island* was my title. Having just read a library book called *Mystery of the Invisible Island,* I was fascinated by the notion of islands and the look of them. Begun at age nine, my book was never completed, even though it was then that I began to think of myself as a writer.

When illness confined me to my bed, books assured that I didn't intrude on the reigning peace and quiet any more than absolutely necessary, like when it was time for a spoonful of cough syrup, or a cup of milk polluted by milk of magnesia, my mother obsessed with the possibility of constipation.

Not completely friendless out in the yard, I had, in addition to flora and fauna camaraderie, one little neighbor friend, Tina, who was younger, shorter, weaker than I. Compliant, she followed my direction, providing me with my first opportunity to wield a little power. I was allowed to play with Tina in my yard but could never go into hers, the unyielding stance of my mother. I think Tina, unlike me, was permitted to stay inside her house, and wasn't always available to come to my yard.

At breakfast, whenever I looked through our kitchen window and saw Tina, I'd be on the edge of my seat, desperate to go play. I'd stop dawdling over the cereal I so disliked, fill my mouth with the soggy stuff, chew, swallow. Running out the door at last, I'd give a loud, ululating call, a signal for Tina to meet me. Divided by a chicken wire fence that ended near the street, our yards came together at the final fencepost, our meeting place, which we called "down by the post."

"Let's look for pretty stones," my customary proposal. Sitting down in the gravel bed separating the street from our front yard grass, we'd poke around in the stones, me keeping an eye on Tina's choices. Occasionally, only occasionally, I'd persuade her to give me one of her discoveries that I found particularly appealing. Once, I remember, Tina balked. I can still visualize the stone in question: 3/4 inch-long, roughly rectangular, shiny black and streaked with silvery quartz. She did not want to give it up. I've long forgotten how many stones I had to sacrifice in exchange to acquire that one small rock, which seemed to have taken on a holy grail magnitude, but get it I did. Perseverance was a mark of my character from the start.

"Hey," I said one day, "what if we go into the woods?" Tina and I had met down by the post and were walking to the back.

"You're not allowed," was Tina's quick comeback.

But I couldn't leave it alone. The woods behind our back yard was enthralling but, by my mother's decree, forbidden. Somehow the fact that Tina was aware of my mother's rules, and that I followed them, was galling.

We were quiet for a few minutes and then...

"I wanna go."

Obedient all summer long, I was bored now. It was late August, school had not started, and the usual outdoor activities held no appeal. I needed something new. *But, oh, I didn't want to get caught!* A momentary fear paralyzed me, and I sat down in the grass, Tina next to me. A small yellow butterfly hovered around some Queen Anne's lace, and then it was gone. As if on cue, I jumped up, suddenly longing to be just as free as that butterfly.

I motioned to Tina, commanding, "Follow me."

We walked along the back fence to its end where a path into the woods began. Scared as I was of my mother, the thrill of adventure emboldened me. I was willing to risk consequences. *The woods.* How desperate I had been to go into it!

"We better remember the way, so we can get back, okay?"

"Yeah."

"So stay on the path, and be careful not to touch any poison ivy," I cautioned as we set off. "You know what it looks like, right?"

"Is that it, there?" she pointed.

"Yes!" No doubt about it—I could see red bumps on the leaves. Then we were quiet, trudging along.

Soon we reached a creek and saw that we had to get across or else retreat. Down a little way from where we stood was a board stretched from one side of the water to the other. Since we didn't know how deep the water was, or whether there were snakes in it, we didn't want to try wading. We both looked at the water, scared.

Tina started crying.

"What's wrong?"

"I don't want to go on that old board. I might fall in." Then, "you go first," Tina said.

Now I felt like crying. But I don't do that, I reminded myself. I'm like a boy, I think, so I don't cry.

"I'm going!" Suddenly bold again, as far as a nine-year-old girl could be, I walked to the crude bridge and put one foot on it, holding my breath. I brought in my other foot, stepped and felt almost as though I were high in the air, instead of a few inches above the brown water.

"It's okay!" I called back to Tina. "Follow me, c'mon, don't worry." I was afraid to look behind me to see if she was coming, afraid I'd lose my balance.

Then I had to talk to myself. *Take another step. It's just a little creek*. I took a step, then saw a ripple. I froze. Waiting for what might come next, I tried to see into the water. Nothing. Probably just some little fish, I thought, but couldn't tell for sure, so I took another step, very cautiously, then two more.

"Tina? Are you behind me?" No answer. "Tina!" Silence. *Oh, no, she's gone!*

"Ti-*na*!!" I yelled. She had left and didn't tell me. I was sure she must have heard me—there was no way she could have gotten very far away so quickly. She was ignoring me while she headed home, I knew, and I was stuck, alone, on a rotting board placed over muddy water. Suddenly I was paralyzed, not wanting to take another step, but reluctant to try to turn around either. Now I did start crying and felt mad at myself for being such a baby.

Finally, I did it, though, turned around, slowly, edging myself into position to backtrack. I stopped crying, realizing I could be happy that I had satisfied my curiosity about the woods, and it was all right to go home. I took another step towards land...and then that old board suddenly slid away from the muddy edge and down I went!

Turned out the creek was shallow, and I found myself in muck, water up to my chest. After sloshing around, I dragged through the creek bottom, got my drenched self onto land. Putting one wet sneaker in front of the other, I stuck to the path and tried not to cry again.

When I emerged from the woods, soaked and spooked, my mother was sitting in a lawn chair. She glared, jumping up to pull me by the arm into the house to the basement.

"Just what did you think you were doing, young lady?!" I hated it when my mother called me that. "You know better than to go into that woods!" Favorite words of hers: *you know better*. Sure, I did. But that didn't mean I didn't *want* to do something; she just couldn't threaten desire out of me.

After a clean-up job and hairbrush retribution, I became an insider, banished to my bedroom for the rest of the day, but in a self-congratulatory spirit for being defiant. Later, I found out that Tina, turned traitor, had confessed where I was when my mother went to her house looking for me.

Cat, rat. I can still see these words on the beginning pages of the McGuffey primer my mother taught me to read from during the first autumn we lived on Pine Road. I see, too, the lighthouse at the end of the book, a black and white image that stayed with me, one conveying solitude and loneliness.

My late afternoon reading sessions were followed by printing practice at a little rolltop desk, so that long before kindergarten I was ready for school. There was no pre-school where we lived, and, once I finally began classes, my reading and writing skills were fairly well established, and I finished lessons quickly. Then I tended to generate a new project, customarily one that utilized crayons, sometimes getting me into trouble.

It was a fascination with those little color sticks that led to my downfall in second grade when Dorothy, my best friend then, was somehow agreeable to a scheme I devised. While some kids were in a reading circle at the front of the classroom, she and I would invade their desks and surreptitiously steal two colors from each kid's crayon box. Only a few students were in the circle at one time and the rest of us were supposed to read at our desks. But what to do when the reading was completed? We were left to our own devices, and mine became stealing. Though I was not a thief by nature, I couldn't resist stockpiling my two favorite crayons, Turquoise and Brilliant Rose, going to great lengths to plunder, if not ships on the high seas as the pirate I had wanted to be, students' desks in our little classroom.

Once Dorothy and I had nabbed whatever crayons we had time to take, I would break each in half, so we could divide the bounty. Our thievery went on for some time, as I recall, and after we had acquired all the available stock, I was excited when someone brought in a brand new box one day, giving me another chance to supplement my cache.

How we managed to go on with this ploy for as long as we did I can't say, but I remember the day we were caught.

The victim was a boy named Jerome and his new crayons were not Crayola but another brand in a large, flat, black and white box. There were no color names, but the desirable shades were easy to spot, and as it was my turn to steal (Dorothy and I alternated). I got what we needed, broke them in half, stashed my pieces and was handing Dorothy hers when I saw the teacher walking towards us. She stopped at our desks, ordered us to get up, then silently led us out of the classroom and into the hall as the other students watched.

"What were you doing?" Mrs. Hosler, a rather stern woman, was not smiling as she questioned us. We didn't answer.

"Well?"

"I don't know," a soft reply from Dorothy.

"Of course, you know," Mrs. Hosler insisted. "And so do I. You took Jerome's crayons. I saw you do it."

My forefinger pressed atop my middle one, I looked up at her. "We didn't mean to," I said lamely.

"How could you *not* mean to?" A reasonable question. Neither Dorothy nor I had an explanation and just stood there waiting for whatever came next.

"Okay, let's see what Mr. McCaughey has to say about it." Taking us both by the hand, she steered us down the hall to the principal's office. He was at his desk and smiled when we entered.

"Mr. McCaughey, I think these girls have something to confess. They had nothing to say to me, but I'm sure they'll tell *you* everything you need to know." We were at his mercy as Mrs. Hosler left.

Maybe we were the first girls to be sent to the principal's office. Usually, boys were the offenders and could expect, in those days, to be swatted with a wooden paddle, but there was a rule against swatting girls, so we got off easily. After confessing our guilt, not without tears, Mr. McCaughey informed us firmly but with a slight smile that he would have to call our parents. I knew, then, that swatting was in my future after all, and an image of my mother's trusty hairbrush made me truly sorry for my criminal behavior.

Sure enough, I took my punishment once again and tried to think about how bad, as I was told, stealing was, and how bad *I* was. Yes, I thought, very bad. But honestly, the attraction of those vibrant colors had been so strong that consequences seemed unimportant; I had only considered how urgently I needed the extra crayons, since I did more coloring than anyone else in the class, which everyone knew, I thought.

The supply of manila paper, plain and graph-style, was seemingly endless and I made good use of it, especially with my designs on the graph paper, sheet after sheet. I pressed the crayons very hard to create bright, shiny squares for every new pattern, and had a great finished collection, which I subsequently divided into two, stapling them and giving one each to the boys I most admired: Bobby and Stanley. Yes, I needed those extra crayons. Would I have taken them otherwise?

I remained obsessed with crayons, could hardly restrain myself from coloring when I finished assigned work pages. The third-grade teacher, Miss Crawley, became exasperated, warning me over and over to keep the crayons in my desk unless she allowed the whole class free time for coloring. But again, if my assignments were done and others were still working, what was I to do? I'd try to read a little, but sometimes I was overcome with the desire to hold a crayon and watch color press into paper. One day I succumbed, my compulsion the last straw for Miss Crawley. So engrossed in design-making that I didn't notice her standing behind my desk, I was startled when her hand suddenly darted out to snatch my box of crayons, and I cringed, knowing I had defied her one time too many.

"I ought to make you *eat* these crayons!" Her fury was evident as she shook the box at me and, terrified, I could imagine my teeth grinding wax. She confiscated the crayons, allowing me to use them from then on only during special projects that required color, which wasn't often. When report cards were sent home that term, my conduct grade in her class was a "U" for unsatisfactory. Moreover, the penned-in mark had been overlaid with a heavy red stroke and sat on the card glaring out, true symbol of Miss Crawley's own scowl, which she awarded me routinely, pleased, I always thought, to do so.

Nothing could dampen my enthusiasm for crayons, not even proof that they weren't magical. I had decided that silver and gold would surely remedy my inability to fly when used for the production of fairy dust, and, forcing the crayons into my pencil sharpener, I ground them to a flaky condition. Longing to join that free spirit Peter Pan in Never-Never Land, I opened my bedroom window, raised the screen, stood on the bed, sprinkled ersatz fairy dust on my shoulders, and jumped! Landing on the floor with a thud, dismayed, though not entirely surprised, I had to acknowledge the limitations of crayons, and closed the window from which I never flew.

Around the same time my school crayons were impounded, I lost my magic box. Our family had gone to my grandparents' house for dinner and, afterwards, my grandmother handed me a green metal art supply box, my father's. He had been a college art major.

"Here," she smiled, "I think you'll be the next artist in the family."

Riding home that night, I sat in the back of the car, so happy with the box in my lap. Once we were in our house, though, my mother announced that it was bedtime, and that I was to place my new treasure in the space under my rolltop desk.

"You can look at it tomorrow," she said, "but not right now. It's late, time to go to sleep."

I put the box away, changed to pajamas, and climbed into bed. Then, when my door was closed, I quietly slid to the floor, whose boards always squeaked a bit, and crawled over to the desk. I had just unclasped the magic box when the door opened and there stood my mother.

"What did I tell you?" she scolded. "Give me that!" She pulled the box away from me and took it to god-knows-what hiding place. Now my crayons were in Miss Crawley's keeping, and my art box had been impounded as well. How was I going to be the next artist in the family as my grandmother had predicted?

The art box remained hidden for a long time. At some point, my mother finally allowed me access to it on occasion, and I must have removed a few of the tools once, squirreling them away. I still have them, though the box itself probably went to the Salvation Army during one of my mother's purging operations.

II.

When I was eleven, my family moved to another house, another neighborhood. As the oldest of three, I more or less continued to function as I had during my only-child period of six years, my younger brother and sister alternately irrelevant and annoying. Early on, my mother frequently charged me with the task of watching my brother when we played outside. From the time he was three or four, I punished him if he didn't do what I told him to do; if my mother spanked me, I hit him in the back. Once, when he was about eight or nine and would not do his homework, I pummeled him to the floor and only let him up when I saw him slightly bleeding on the carpet. Though I've carried no appreciable amount of guilt through life, what I do have stems partly from this violence of mine, which underscores the undeniable fact that we can all be led into cruel and brutal behavior if trained or influenced at an early age.

It was unimaginable to me that anyone other than *I* could be my father's favorite. Strangely I thought, my sister (I found out years later) had had the same illusion. Whatever the truth of the matter, our father, despite his flaws, was *our* favorite. He was extremely favored, too, by some of the neighborhood kids.

"Can Nanners come out and play," a little French American boy from down the street would ask when we answered his knock at the door. My father's comical nickname had originated from a mispronunciation—*Nannerhardt*—of our last name Engelhardt, which evolved to *Nanners*, then the further-shortened *Nans,* preferred by the boy next door.

Nans. His popularity grew from his willingness to throw baseballs, play croquet, or just generally hang out on the porch with any kid who came by. A game we gleefully played on summer evenings was one we called "The Charlie Game," which my father had devised. He would sing, "Life is just a bowl of Charlies," so we sang verses from well-known songs and substituted *Charlie* for a key word. Absurd, but endlessly entertaining for all of us. Years later a memory of the game inspired my poem, given honorable mention in a journal's contest:

> Letter from K on a Drunken Raft
>
> Dear Charlie,
> I write to you from Flux, the sea of a sea-
> blue funk that flows through middle ages. I float
> like Quetzlcoatl on a raft of snakes & flaunt
> my malice & pique that rain on your jamboree.
>
> I'm on my way, I'm on my way, I'm K.
> Yet castles seem to fade to a check-point, Charlie–
> your boot, your bluff, your global hurly-burly.
> This floating's a helluva job & what does it pay?
>
> The Bald, the Bad, the Bold, the Fat & the Simple.
> Sometimes a Wise, a Well-beloved, or a Great,
> but I can't remember the deeds, the conquests, the fate
> of a single Charles, or if anyone had a dimple.
>
> But they all came to my bedroom, every one.
> I fêted them in all their coronations,
> jollied myself through so many mutilations,
> took every bloody kiss as sine qua non.

> Great pretender, pumping iron on the throne,
> you're a little tramp, Charlie, full of holes.
> Charlie, you're vile, you stink of fleurs du mal
> & what could you know of real murder, my Chan?
>
> You're a snake in Brown's clothing, egghead charm
> the best disarming tactic, but I'll survive.
> That kind of ruse can only feed my drive
> to be among the fittest, dear old Charles.
>
> I could modulate to a Larry, Moe, Curley,
> but I'll sail to the true eye of this letter: life
> (we used to sing back home in Cincinnati)
> is just a bowl of Charlies.   Signed, your wife.

That my father was so popular with kids was a feather in my own cap, I thought. Nobody's father could quite measure up to mine, and, therefore, *nobody's-as-special-as-I* went my reasoning. That he had won first and second prize, house and car, in a puzzle-solving contest, which no other father I knew had done, fine-tuned his cachet.

The halcyon days of summer with my father were, however, intersewn now and then with stormy ones. He might go out on a Saturday morning for a haircut, or a Thursday night for golf, and never come back, at least not until the wee hours of the next morning, inebriated, angry, belligerent, disinclined to simply pass out in bed. The darkness that hung over my father complicated him, though, added interest, so that even while I suffered terribly when he binged, I was all the more convinced of his preeminence. Of course, that stance was predicated by the fact that no one spoke of a family's closet skeletons in those days, so there was a mystique about my father. Little did I know that his propensity to over-drink was not unique, and that the father of one of my close girlfriends was probably an even heavier drinker.

Considering my father's drinking a curse that sullied the core of family life, my mother was ashamed of it, hid it from the few people with whom she occasionally socialized. Consequently, I concealed it also and had a horror of anyone's finding out about it. At the same time, I would look up, surreptitiously, words in the dictionary: *alcoholic, inebriated, soused, loaded, blotto, stupor, liquor, whiskey, spirits*...any word I came upon that was affiliated with *drunk*. Seeing the words in print, reading the definitions, had the same effect, I suppose, as watching a scary movie: the riveting combination of fear, repulsion, and fascination.

In addition to haircuts and golf games gone bad, there were the New Year's Eve and 4th of July calamities. On these occasions, my father often seized the opportunity to down god-knows-how-many Manhattans or Pabst Blue Ribbons, his favorite quaffs at the time. The summer I was sixteen, in particular, I remember. As the eldest, commissioned to babysit for my brother and sister so my parents could go out, I was home on 4th of July night when I might have gone out myself, and, anxious throughout the evening, I couldn't read, didn't want to go to bed. Even if I could have slept, I would be awakened, I knew, by some kind of end-of-the-night strife, so I stayed up, lounging around on the couch, listening to the radio, until I heard the car.

Our narrow driveway went down to a garage beneath the living room window facing the street and my father always backed down when he put the car away each night, something he had trouble with when he had been drinking. Many times, from my bedroom directly above the living room, I could hear him backing partway down, pulling up, re-positioning, trying again, always with loud gunning of the motor, jerky movements. This time I heard the car stop and a door slam. I ran upstairs to my bedroom to peek out of the window, seeing my father hadn't even attempted the driveway, since the car was in front of the house. My father, lurching, was following my mother to the front door. I lay down on my bed to await what was sure to be a fracas.

Soon there was the usual stomping through the house and raised voices whose words I couldn't make out, but this time seemed worse than usual. I have no memory of how I knew my mother had picked up a kitchen knife, but somehow it happened, and I knew it.

Ultimately, it was all a fizzle, and no one got hurt. During the scuffle, though, unable to bear it that night, I sneaked downstairs and out the front door, making my way half a mile or so down the road to my boyfriend Dick's house. Once I got there, I didn't know what to do. It was still dark in the very early morning, not a time to be ringing someone's doorbell, so I crouched down in the bushes in front of the house and waited, uncomfortably, until the sun started to rise. Then, nervous, I rang the bell, shamefaced as I explained my abrupt appearance. I was greeted kindly, though, and I spent some time sitting on the sofa with Dick, facing the front window. I noticed a car going by the house a couple of times, my aunt and uncle, looking for me I suppose. But they didn't park and come to the door, and I stayed hidden in the house.

In keeping with my mother's secretiveness about the drinking escapades, there was my father's morning-after pretense that nothing untoward had taken place. And if he suffered hangovers, no one would have known it; reinstalled as his charming, if acerbic, self, he'd go about his day as usual. My mother, though, would be sulky, and I ...I would feel cut to the bone. But silent, powerless.

There were times when my mother used me to scuttle any impulse my father had to go drinking. He'd say he was going to get a haircut on a Saturday morning, and she'd send me with him. That he had, in fact, gone for haircuts and not come back, warranted these tactics, which, I suspect, my father resented. Of course, I felt self-conscious in the barber shop, but reassured that my father would not be drunk that day, since he couldn't take me to a bar. Once, when our car needed to be inspected, she sent me and my siblings with him. It was nighttime and the only inspection station in town was rather far from our home, in an area well known to my father, where he'd be sure to find a bar and run into old buddies.

After the very early years of my parents' marriage, when my father had *settled down* somewhat (a phrase used by both my mother and grandmother), the drinking episodes were fewer. That meant, though, that I'd be waiting for the next one, dreading the thought of it, increasingly nervous as time passed, knowing another bout was inevitable and probably imminent.

My father's devil-be-damned drinking, his center-of-neighborhood-attention and domination of dinner-table conversations where he related the events of his day at the office, told jokes, analyzed the behavior of fellow-workers, and recounted–play by play–golf matches and lunch-time chess games were all indicators of an extreme solipsism. In our family my father, thoroughly self-involved, outshone (then out-rusted) everyone else. But my mother's sovereignty in the household was absolute. She ruled, petulantly, punitively. Kept on a short leash and an allowance, just enough for cigarettes, my father had to hand her his paycheck, for fear that he might blow it all at the racetrack, which early in the marriage he had done. And, filthy or not, he, too, like us children, had to bathe in the basement.

I loved it when my father sang "Nature Boy," popularized by Nat King Cole in the 1940s. His tenor tones tremoloed the lines:

> *There was a boy,*
> *A very strange enchanted boy*
> *They say he wandered very far, very far*
> *Over land and sea*
> *A little shy*
> *And sad of eye*
> *But very wise*
> *Was he...*

Intrigued by notions of strangeness, enchantment, wandering, and being a little shy, a little sad, I was that nature *boy*, within, being a little less girl than other girls, I felt.

With a good ear and a flair for imitation, my father sang plenty of other songs around the house, echoing the likes of not only Cole, but also icons such as Frank Sinatra, Dean Martin, Sammy Davis, Jr., and Tony Bennett. His love for the music enveloped me, although I never embraced pop music as enthusiastically as he did. Sometimes my mother sang, too, but I can't associate any specific lyrics with her; the music I think of is classical, instrumental, two works standing out in my memory: "Liebestraum" by Franz Liszt and Manuel de Falla's "Ritual Fire Dance." She'd play recordings of both. I remember hearing the fire dance sometimes, volume turned high, as she did her baking.

Throughout my teen years, a little blue radio sat by my bed, and I listened to a certain station before falling asleep at night. While there were singers and songs I liked, I was never carried away by either, so my attention to pop, rock, blues, jazz, folk, and classical music was casual. I thoroughly disliked country-western and gospel, the former for what I felt was a whiny sound and inane words, the latter because of my antipathy towards religion and anything that derived from it.

American culture is such that a teenager would have to live a more hermetic life than I did to escape witnessing something about trends in music. I confess that as a seventh grader, I bought a magazine that had a spread on Elvis Presley; it was the one time that my curiosity got the better of me, the one time I bought any kind of *fan* magazine. It was hard to discount the Elvis hoopla that was already mounting in his early years, but after checking out him and his music, I concluded that neither held any appeal for me, and prided myself on being largely immune to his husky-sexy tones and grinding motions.

Little snob that I was, I became quite proficient at sneering, and a 1959 outdoor concert I attended with boyfriend Dick engendered an incredulity I had never known. It was all about girls in the audience fainting when the headliner, Fabian, came to the stage. Surely, I thought, it was because of the July heat. Later I considered the possibility that they had been paid for their swooning. Well, I wish, yeah, I wish they had been paid, but I doubt it.

The only other concert I went to in my jeering youth featured Conway Twitty of "It's Only Make Believe" fame. His name alone was somehow off-putting to me. The song title pretty much sums up my outlook on pop music: nothing of it represents the *real*. Some guy singing on a stage, or recording a song, pouring out angst-ridden tones and lyrics about love lost, while the same guy probably screwed around so much that whatever girl he might have professed to love had finally dumped him. Or the opposite scenario: after said profession of love, some new girl came along, and he dumped the old one. And to myself I always said *so what, who cares.* I would not have *my* character, *my* life, defined by such love stuff, or pay undue attention to the music that epitomized it.

Although I'd hear songs here and there, mostly on radio, TV, or, later in bars, I often didn't register who the singer was, with such commanding exceptions as Sinatra, Presley, McCartney, those kind of forced-down-your-throat super-celebs. I *heard* the songs. I did not *listen* to them. Never knew many of the words, often did not know the titles or performers. The fatuous lyrics made little impression on me. A 1960s song whose sound I liked appalled me years later when I happened to hear it and picked up on some of the words: *do the things he likes to do/ wear your hair just for him ('cause wishin' and hopin' won't get you into his arms).* I was shocked at myself, that I never, in all the times I had heard them, considered the import of the words, and dumbfounded at the degree to which I had been so dismissive, by tendency, not design. This song, whose sound I had so enjoyed, sung by a woman, ended with, *all you gotta do is hold him and kiss him and squeeze him and love him, yeah, just do it and after you do, you will be his.* Yeah, *do it,* and you'll be his. 'Til he doesn't want you any more, or until he wants to *do it* with someone else. And who, I thought, wants to be some guy's possession anyway?

Then the Beatles arrived. I was smitten! Aside from two albums, though, I never acquired any of their music, did not even become familiar with all of it. During my sophomore year in college, on a shopping trip we took together, my grandmother Eva bought me *Meet the Beatles*; a few years later I received as a gift *Sgt. Pepper's Lonely Hearts Club Band.* It simply didn't occur to me, when I was younger, to invest the few discretionary dollars I had in records, and it was happenstance that I wound up with a few albums, gifts or borrowed (permanently) from a boyfriend intent on introducing me to his favorites: Joan Baez; Peter, Paul, and Mary; Nancy Wilson; Johnny Mathis; Ethel Ennis. Only after marriage did I begin to randomly buy a few albums, then tapes, CDs, finally downloads for an iPod.

It would be many years before I could enjoy Sinatra's singing, much as I loved my father's imitations. By the time I was able to listen, by choice, to the songs, Sinatra had died, my father's death preceding his by a year and a half. My pleasure in the music even then was largely occasioned by memories, not the smart-ass or world-weary tones of Sinatra himself. I listened to songs like "My Way" and "In the Wee Small Hours of the Morning," two favorites, simultaneously reading, in succession, four biographies of the man, for whom I felt some strange kind of fondness, as my father's very being seemed so infused with his. Nonetheless, both were deeply flawed characters, Sinatra's blemishes succinctly expressed by one biographer, Arnold Shaw: "Sinatra...was frequently an explosive porcupine of ill-temper...couldn't help using his fists and four-letter words in public."

An integral part of the mid-60s gang known as the "Rat Pack" (along with fellow singer/comedians Dean Martin, Peter Lawford, Sammy Davis, Jr., and Joey Bishop), Sinatra was something of a role model for my father, who told me during the crumbling of his marriage that he had a "project to hurt people" and to be "as rotten as I can," i.e., be a *rat*. I'm only marginally acquainted, I'm sure, with the successes of his venture.

"It was no accident that he came to specialize in songs of loss, longing and survival," Shaw wrote about Sinatra. And it was no accident that my father sang those songs through what must have been the angst of his married years. "Nobody knows what I've suffered," he said to me shortly after divorce.

In spite of my dismissiveness, inattentiveness, music has been as important to me, perhaps, as to anyone else in American society, particularly *sound* rather than *words*, solo classical piano works affecting me more than anything else. And I can play a little, which makes for a richer experience– Chopin, Debussy, Rachmaninoff, Scriabin, et al. In equal standing with piano music, though, is silence. I must have abundant silence, time during the course of a day to hear no voices, no cars, no bustling in the world.

In my head, I hear the melody of a song now and its three key words: *silence is golden*. All the other words, who sang it, wrote it, and when? I don't know.

HOME AGAIN

I'm going home again, to Cincinnati, my place of birth, childhood, and a few adulthood years.

"Don't you know you can't go home again?" Australian journalist Ella Winter said to Thomas Wolfe, who got her permission to turn the question into a book title for his novel, *You Can't Go Home Again,* published posthumously in 1940.

I know you can't go home again. Not if you expect the place to be the same, look or feel exactly the same as it did when it was yours. But I don't. In fact, I have trained myself to have no, at most low, expectations in this state called life, and the place was never mine anyway, not fully, not the way a place is when you have important things to do in it, know many people, some of them very well, feel you belong there. I think you call a place *home* when your engagement with people, and living, is ample and, you believe, significant.

From my current home in Texas, an indirect route to Cincinnati brings me to Gatlinburg in the Smoky Mountains of Tennessee, a spot I feel compelled to revisit. I pull into the parking lot of a place called a *motor lodge*; still standing after more than eighty years, this establishment was first called a *hotel*, then dubbed a *new hotel* in 1953 when my grandparents brought my family here. Definitely modest and motor-lodgish now, the front is only vaguely familiar, but what I remember more clearly, and still have a photo of, is the lawn in the back where my brother and I lounged in hammocks.

As I enter the lobby, I notice framed pictures hanging on the walls, a few of which show the place as it was in the fifties. I'm not sure why, but I take photos of the photos, then check in and walk the long dismal hallways to my room. I see it looks very clean, and I'm staying just one night, so I deposit bags and set out to walk the tourist-clogged streets while it's still light. On the way out, I wander first to the back of the lodge where I linger at a window to look out, not on a lovely lawn, but a street, and beyond it another hotel. No hammocks here.

Joining vacationing hordes on the main thoroughfare, I trudge along, finally turning down a side street to come upon a tucked-away shop that sells things made in Ireland. I get the idea to honor the memory of my grandmother by buying something that will remind me of her and our long-ago visit here. Since her heritage was Scotch-Irish, I expect this store to have just the thing, but once inside, going up and down aisles and studying the goods, I'm reminded of how I dislike buying souvenir trinkets, which are mostly gimcrack, and just more stuff to safeguard or discard. Resolved, however, I finally stop in front of a glass case, peer into it, and there it is...

"Could I see that necklace?" I ask the shopkeeper, pointing to a small silver fairy with blue-gemmed wings.

He smiles. "Sure."

Fingering this fantastical silver form, I goad myself and me: *Buy the goddamned thing!* I open my purse and pull out a credit card.

"You don't need to wrap it. I'll just wear it." And, around a reluctantly obedient neck, I loop and fasten the chain, anointing my fairy as muse.

At last, I'm settling into a rented room, opening various bags, putting things in closet and drawers and on the desk my new landlord procured for me, when I see one in the unoccupied room next to mine.

"There's no outlet here," I say to him, pointing to the bare wall after desk and chair are in place.

"You want one there?"

By afternoon I'm plugging in computer and printer, arranging books, getting ready to write. I have two months here in this hideaway to launch whatever my project turns out to be. I sit down, stare at my laptop, white screen as bedeviling as any blank sheet of paper. I stroke the wings of my fairy. C'mon, make your silver self useful, be museful!

The buses aren't orange anymore. But telephone poles, doubling as bus stops, do still have orange bands painted round the rough wood, the one I waited at more than sixty years ago still standing by the railroad tracks. From first grade through fifth, I took a Cincinnati city bus to school, and my father caught an earlier one to get downtown to his job at the Bureau of Internal Revenue. *Bureau of Internal Revenue.* I never knew what that meant in the world; to me, it meant he got home by six, when he chose to come home.

One morning–I must have been about seven–my father, ever punctual but having awakened late, had to take the same bus I rode to school. Though I pretended I wasn't watching, I could see his long-legged stride, so distinctive, as he crossed the street. Dressed in a coat and hat, customary garb of white-collar men in the fifties, he slowly walked up to where I was already standing, shivering in the cold. I refused to look at him. He didn't speak. The bus came and I boarded, taking a seat close to the front. My father followed, going to the back, wise and aware, I think. As he was passing by I raised my angry face and saw his smile was a smirk, as it was so often. I couldn't use that word then, and couldn't have said he was *defiant*, but I remember the caliber of that smile, on the bus where we sat, far apart.

These are the things I recall, no specific details about the night before, a night that must have been like many other nights during those years we lived near the bus stop. Nights when my father didn't arrive home at six, when by seven my mother gave me supper, so I sat down to eat, but she, sullen, didn't. And later, after sleeping for a few hours, I'd awaken and watch the movement of light from an occasional passing car, against the wall and ceiling as I lay on my back, straining to hear muffled but clearly hostile voices.

Through the years the same fatherless suppers recurred periodically, the same wee-hour arrivals, and as I grew older I couldn't even fall asleep when I anticipated the staggering, door-slamming, and vehemence of my parents' quarrel. In a conversation I once had with my mother years later, she described me as a child with a "worrisome nature." I guess I was.

Orange. A color insistent, not to be ignored. My mother was best represented by an angry orange, her stripes the black ones of depression. Fierce, solitary, territorial, she was a tiger. As Hindu deities that have their various avatars, she had assumed a human form but remained, essentially, tiger, her territory the house, which she had made into a home, *her* home, not my father's or mine. We were expected to be proper guests, and with much coaching learned how to behave as such, never disturbing the arrangement of furniture and knick-knacks. Obedient, we made no messes, carefully drying the sink after rinsing our assigned water glasses. My father carried his beanbag-bottomed ashtray room to room, emptying it frequently, so that the decorative living room trays remained as ash-free and shiny as scoured bathtubs. There was hell to pay for any deviation from the mandates, tiger-tongue lashings the least of them, hairbrush spanking for me. When all was cleaned, washed, ironed, cooked, baked, my mother would retreat to the kitchen table with tea and cigarettes, a book propped up before her.

There was no spot in the house not subject to my mother's fervid, purposeful hands. So when it wound up blood-stained, my underwear, I hid it in a doll cradle beneath a little satin cover. I don't know what I was thinking.

"You're disgusting! How could you put this filthy thing in here?" my mother upbraided me. Had I put it in the laundry hamper, though, the same lambasting, no doubt, would have resulted. Not creating filth was the only acceptable deportment in my mother's home.

No coffee klatsches, no tea parties, no glasses of wine in late afternoon with a neighbor ever took place in our house. My mother did not indulge in lunch table commiserations with friends, neither did she volunteer for any organization, join a single club. And no church ladies called on her. Areligious, non-churchgoing, she was, nonetheless, cloistered as a nun. I'm sure the hermitic tendencies originated in a shyness she once acknowledged and what she described as a lonely, dismal childhood, her father having died when she was a baby.

Mother stayed with her grandparents, her one sister with an aunt, as their mother worked at menial jobs to support them. Living as an only child, then, with a diabetic, blind grandmother and a mean, crotchety grandfather, she rarely saw anyone else. As a young girl, she helped care for the grandmother, was subject to threats from the grandfather.

"See that building," this Quaker Dutchman would say, according to my mother, pointing to an orphanage they rode by when they traveled by bus to go shopping, "that's where you're going if you don't behave!"

I have no sense that my mother was ever a very bad or difficult child, though I can imagine she was habitually sullen. Her occasional admonishment to me was "wipe that pout off your face"; my guess is that she, herself, often heard those very words. Judging by her adult behavior, though, which was so reclusive, controlled, organized, and bookish, my mother was probably quietly obedient during childhood. And that's what she wanted me to be. Our weekly trips to local libraries, after she began teaching me to read at three and a half, set me up for the quiet life.

Courtesy of books, then, I was as good as absent, silent, trying not to engender any filth.

In contrast to my mother's childhood, my father's included, I speculate, a lot of babying. Youngest of three, his father's favorite, when growing up he sported an abbreviation of his full name Richard Daniel: the silly but endearing *Dicky-Dan*.

When we lived with Grandma and Poppy, my father's parents, my mother once protested to her father-in-law about one of my father's late-night drunken returns.

"This is his house, and he can do what he wants," was Poppy's reply.

Sensing that my parents were both angry, but too young at first to understand the sources of anger, I finally began to piece together bits of their histories, respective characters, and behaviors to form, in all likelihood, accurately, a rationale for that wholesale anger, which, like any good ghost, did a fine haunting of our house. At the core of this anger was me, product of premarital sex, for my cousin confirmed, long after I had reached adulthood, that I was an 8-month baby. Since "out of wedlock" was the most pejorative label assigned to a birth in 1944, my parents had a "wedding occasioned or precipitated by pregnancy"–i.e., "shotgun wedding." Though no one ever spoke to me about the situation, needless to say, I suspect that my father was unhappy about it, and my mother had high expectations for a more comfortable life than she had experienced growing up. Her hopes were dashed from the start, and she once confessed to me that when I was a year old she went to her mother and complained.

"This marriage isn't working."

"You made your bed, lie in it," was the trite, uncharitable reply. "No one has ever divorced in this family, and you're not going to be the first."

So they endured. My father tolerated his unhappiness until he couldn't, then binged, heedless of any effects his behavior had on others. Home being the only thing she could control, my mother ran her tight ship, displacing much of her anger on first me, then my brother and sister.

If I could color my family, I'd choose orange, a color that connects to the word *anger*, their common letters, *a-n-g-e*.

Anger

In slices with the bread   in pats with butter
   in vats, you might say
      after much stomping, purple
         as an apoplectic aspect
Aged   uncorked often
romping with kids   curled around dog's tail
   in corners in place of dust—
      o never any dust in corners!
Hanging in folds of formal drapes
rustling like crinoline & taffeta
tiptoe-sneaky   nimble   hellbent
   orange as pumpkin   red as wagon
round   square & perpendicular
   to every stick & stone
present   pluperfect   future
  perfect as the 50s were thought to be
animal   vegetable   mineral & percolating
              with the coffee
In stacks of mail & magazine racks
   banded with the evening news
      straight up   on the rocks   & skewed
Sunbright   usual as high noon in June
   hard & cold as porcelain   stainless steel
         or nose of mother
Casual   stammering   eloquent   simmering
  redolent of musk   melon   grass
     beer-foamy   yeasty & massive as a yak
insinuating itself into every half-a-laugh
   crevicing mouth   brow   fist
     worming its fat-cyst-self
   where nothing else would go
Off to work in overcoat
     staying home in apron
Going off & on like birthday candle flicker
   almost beautiful, the flickering
almost sweet   sweet as cake   layered
    just like cake
   seemingly good to eat   It became

>   what has to be
> has to be called *scrumptious*
>   So we ate & ate & ate

By chance, I'm staying in a city within the city of Cincinnati: Norwood, where my parents grew up, where I began life. My rented room is in a house just off Montgomery Road, the main street in Norwood, and as I drive along I come to the library, small but imposing with its Italian Renaissance design, one of many my mother frequented. But something doesn't look right here.

I park, and as I walk toward the steps, I can almost feel the tight grip of a hand on mine, my mother ushering me to the children's section. While she searched the adult shelves, I'd sit on a dark wooden bench against the window looking at books, my favorite, *East of the Sun and West of the Moon*. Reminiscent of *Beauty and the Beast*, it featured a white bear, a beautiful girl, and personified winds: north, south, east, west.

Once inside, I see the bench is still there, but I'm here now as a grownup for the first time, so I take a chair at a table and open my laptop, thinking how the last time I was in this space there were no personal computers, and the term *laptop* didn't exist. Researching the library, I find a photo of it in the early years, the caption showing it had been built in 1907. Now I understand what looked odd from the outside: in the picture, two front yard trees, taller than the building, soften the aspect; trees that are gone. I read that a 1965 remodeling job hid many of the building's original features, and in 2001 another renovation restored its earlier charm. Maybe the trees went in 1965, replaced by some much smaller, less imposing bushes, which scarcely mitigate the nakedness, so startling.

I leave the library and continue on to the first home I can remember, my grandparents' house on Glenside Avenue. The houses look much the same, though the street is no longer lined with sycamores whose peeling bark and distinctive leaf-shape I remember, as well as the smell of fall leaves burning after my grandfather had raked them into piles. Has Norwood chopped down every last tree, I wonder? The storybook houses, some with turrets, are small to begin with and look even smaller in these barren surroundings, and, of course, from my adult perspective.

Through the years, when I'd return to Cincinnati for short visits, I'd sometimes come to this street, gaze at the red brick house with its stone arched doorway, front windows of leaded glass. The telephone number here was Jefferson 0938. Why I remember that is inexplicable, since I don't think I ever called the number, and my grandparents relinquished it when they moved to a different part of the city in 1958. Memory—what a strange, tentacled and miserly animal, hanging on to so many inconsequential scraps.

Does the basement here still have a separate room we called the *rathskeller*? If so, do the people living here still call it that? Despite all the intervening years, my image of that room is sharp, certain things standing out in particular: an old floor model Victrola that had to be cranked up to play the record that seemed to live on its turntable, "Yes, We Have No Bananas," a song from 1923. And on a chair there were my father's charcoal drawings of nude women, produced when he was a university art student.

I suppose I'm not the first person to sit in front of an old residence and briefly consider ringing the doorbell. *Could I see your house?* I'd say. *I once lived here with my grandparents and used to play in the rathskeller. I won't stay long; I'm not a robber…* . There are those, I guess, who would march right up the steps, and make such a plea; I'm not, however, one of them. I just sit in my car looking at the house, thinking of my grandmother, butter mints, and peppermint ice cream, her favorites.

Cincinnati, by the Ohio River (called Oh-he-yo, or Great River, by locals), was first named Losantiville in 1788. Renamed two years later after the Society of the Cincinnati, by its president, General Arthur St. Clair, the city's name ultimately comes from Roman dictator/farmer Lucius

Quintus Cincinnatus (568–430 BCE). When called upon, Cincinnatus agreed to be temporary dictator of Rome when it was under siege. Leading the army, in fifteen days he saved Rome, returning then to the plowing of his field, admired ever after for his simple life and lack of ambition. "The center of all my enjoyments is the home wherein are my wife and children," he said, "and I have no wish to wander out from that home in pursuit of any pleasures that the world presents." Singular fellow.

Cincinnati, a city with many nicknames, including *Cincy* and *The Queen City*, the latter from "Catawba Wine," circa 1857, by Henry Wadsworth Longfellow, who ended his poem with,

> And this Song of the Vine,
> This greeting of mine,
> The winds and the birds shall deliver,
> To the Queen of the West,
> In her garlands dressed,
> On the banks of the Beautiful River.

At that time, Cincinnati was the largest city west of the east coast.

Cincinnati. Known, too, as *Porkopolis* when its pork-packing industry in the mid to late 1800s was a cornerstone of the city's prosperity. By 1890, it was also the leading carriage and wagon center of the world, where its shops were producing half of all the vehicles built in the country.

Cincinnati. Home of the *Big Red Machine*. Founded in 1866, winning every game it played in 1869, baseball's first openly all-professional team was originally called the *Red Stockings,* then shortened to the *Reds* in the 1890s, acquiring its *machine* nickname when it dominated baseball's National League from 1970 to 1976.

Cincinnati. Home of *Big Joe*, a 35,000-pound bell with a 640-pound clapper. Seven feet tall with a nine-foot diameter, it's the largest swinging bell ever cast in the U.S. In 1895, it took fourteen horses to haul it from foundry to St.

Francis De Sales church, where it still hangs in its tower. After the inaugural ring produced deafening vibrations as far away as fifteen miles, it was decreed that it remain immobile forever and is rung now only by tapping its rim with a foot hammer. *Big Joe,* named for its largest donor, parishioner Joseph T. Buddeke, combines *Joseph* and *Big Ben,* London's Westminster bell.

Cincinnati. A deeply conservative city with one of the highest rates of income inequality, where one wealthy suburb was second only to Manhattan's Upper East Side in donations to the Republican campaign of 2004.

Cincinnati. Despite its history of being an important stop for the Underground Railroad, the city has been called the most, or one of the most, racist cities in the country.

Cincinnati. A good place to leave if you are not conservative, religious, racist, and/or not a baseball fan. "When the end of the world comes, I want to be in Cincinnati because it's always twenty years behind the times" is a quote often attributed to—but not proven to be so—Mark Twain.

Cincinnati, a name I like for the sound and its letters. A name I once hated to say though, city I didn't want to be from, because I knew it was not New York, or San Francisco, London, Paris...not a city of any real interest, I thought.

I'm driving along, noting buildings and houses, landmarks and signs, I try to accurately register what I feel: excitement, contentment, nostalgia, regret, sorrow... . The usual fluctuation of feelings when I return to this city. Am I home? Is a place of birth and coming of age always home, no matter where you go, how many times you relocate, how many different houses you live in, how many years have passed? Is it to be called *home,* the city I always wanted to leave? Or is home a current city, lived in for thirty-six consecutive years? Maybe I'm homeless in some essential way.

Landmarks are not the same, though there is an ongoing familiarity of place. Some buildings no longer exist or have been significantly changed, but streets still wind and slope in the same old ways. I come to the crest of a hill and remember that very long ago a small ice cream shop called *Creamy Whip* once sat there, gone now. And yet that rise up the hill along a street whose name is the same—Montgomery—summons a memory: my mother, father, Uncle Buddy, and I stopping on a summer evening for ice cream cones, all of the adults following their indulgence with a cigarette as I continue licking ice cream whipped to unusual creaminess, a new concoction back then.

Names resonate deeply with me, perhaps more than sights. Street names, imprinted on my psyche in a way no other names seem to be, spark the feeling of lost-home: Blue Ash, Pine, Sycamore, Lamont, Kenwood, Plainfield, Montgomery. The combinations of letters, the look and sound of these names, significance of place, memory of riding with my parents along the roads—all engender a strong feeling of affinity. But none of the associations I have with the names are relevant now. I don't drive on Blue Ash to get to a house where I live with my parents; I don't pass through Deer Park and Silverton on my way to Norwood, on Montgomery Road to Quatman, then Fenwick, then Glenside to go see my grandmother and grandfather, have dinner with the extended family, parents, aunts and uncles laughing together. The houses are there on Glenside, but the people are gone, my grandparents and their neighbors, whose names I can still recall: Coclough, Dean, Talmadge.

I drive to my parents' first house on Pine Road. There's a chicken wire fence now around the entire yard, which has a clutter of trikes and bikes and a plastic pool. Green and white metal awnings hang over the front door, windows, and side porch and the breezeway is enclosed. A sign over the garage reads "Paw Paw's Garage." The only recognizable tree, the front maple, has grown very tall, and the woods behind the house? Gone. Another area of houses having taken over. In general, the homes in this modest neighborhood have been well cared for, surviving as neat, trim cottages. Only this, my former one, displeases me. No, you can't go home again.

    I drive on. A few houses down the street is the site where at age eleven I had my one significant accident. Riding on the back of a bike steered by Timmy, a classmate, from my house to my friend Sandy's house, I instinctively pulled my leg in towards the bike as a car passed. Instantly, my foot got caught in the spokes, bike crashing to the concrete with Timmy and me. Sandy stopped her own bike, got off, and ran into her house across the street to get her mother, who arrived fairly quickly, though it seemed forever, pain distorting all sense of time. Unable to free my foot, in agony, all I could do was steel myself, loath to begin crying in front of a boy. A wire cutter finally loosened the spoke, and I pulled out my foot with a bruised, almost mangled ankle, which to this day has a scarred indentation.

    Examination at the doctor's office showed my ankle had not been sprained or broken, but the trauma and bruising, extensive, made crutches necessary. All this was bad enough, but my physical pain was matched by another wretchedness a couple of days later.

    For a time during the 1950s our evening newspaper, *The Cincinnati Post*, sponsored puzzle contests that required significant work to complete since they ran for ninety days, which meant ninety puzzles to solve, their difficulty increasing day by day. My father, lover of puzzles, had entered several times, winning from an extensive range of prizes a lamp, a set of silverware, and five dollars twice. In 1955, the contest, called "Whozit," was based on silhouettes of well-known people, each one accompanied by a hint and nine names from which to choose; contestants were required to write a tie-breaking jingle, "Why I like *The Cincinnati Post*." My father, having spent hours and hours at various local libraries (during this pre-computer time) researching names and hints for the later, hard-to-identify silhouettes, submitted six entries (there was no limit) and two of them were the same.

The day after my bike mishap, the phone rang, and my mother answered it. On the other end, a man from the *Post* informed her that she and my father were "Whozit" winners. My father's two identical entries were the only perfect ones, in his name and in my mother's, respectively, the latter judged to have the better jingle. My mother had won first prize, a house; my father, second prize, a car. The paper's front-page article announced the surprising news:

> Fantastic, almost unbelievable, but it actually happened. The $15,000 home and the 1955 Ford, top prizes in The Post's $20,000 Whozit contest, were won by husband and wife.... It's fantastic for among the thousands of entries submitted only two were perfect.
> "It's such a shock I can hardly talk," said Mrs. Engelhardt when *The Post* informed her of the windfall. She was so nervous she tore two pairs of nylons while dressing to have her picture taken.

And there they are on the front page of the newspaper, my father—hammering a "For Sale" sign in our front yard—my mother, my brother, my sister. And where in the photo am I? A photographer had come to take pictures for the news story, no family having won the top two prizes in the history of the *Post's* contests, and had snapped photos inside our house and out in the yard. In the middle of the session, I had to leave, hobbling out on my crutches to get into Sandy's car, so her mother could drive us to a girl scout outing. But I had been confident that the picture selected for the front page would be one that included me—how could it be otherwise? Wouldn't the newspaper people want the *entire* family in the picture? When the paper was delivered the next evening, there I was: missing. I was desolate.

Right now, I'm sitting in front of Sandy's house, and I see that the house next to it, quite appealing, is for sale by owner.

Someone pulls into the driveway, and I get out of my car to greet a man who is, indeed, the owner.

"I'd like to see your house." *Why*, I wonder?

"Come on in."

I follow the owner up the front steps and into a living room. No entry hall, little space, but neat and clean and sweet.

"If you want to buy the house and are interested," the guy says, "we'll leave the furniture. We're going on the road in our RV, so we can't take much with us."

He introduces me to his wife Kandy and we all sat down to talk. I told them I had grown up on the street, that their house was next door to my girlfriend's house, and that I was engaged in a writing project. As the conversation continued, it emerged that Kandy had a twin sister named Sandy...*No!*

"It's too coincidental," I told them. "My friend Sandy who lived next door had a sister, not a twin, though, named Kandy!"

What are the chances of meeting up so many years down the road with these same names, *Kandy* spelled the same way, that I remember from next door? A complete non-believer in destiny, fate, kismet, and karma, an adherent of coincidence and the random, nonetheless, as thoughts hopped through my mind with black-tailed jackrabbit speed, I couldn't help but think it was somehow ordained that I buy this house in Sandy-Kandy Land.

Suddenly–*why not?* Why not have this house for a retreat instead of renting a room again if I want to return to Cincinnati while writing whatever it is I'm writing. I'd always have a place to stay. I could move right in and not worry about furnishing the place and I could take my time on memory lane, lingering wherever I wished for as long as necessary.

Reader, I bought it. The little house on Pine Road in Sandy-Kandy Land.

Holiday time on Pine Road. I have made a long journey from the early Christmases of my life, filled with eagerness, then excitement, to a place of surfeit, indifference. Passing through childhood, then the years of my own child-raising, which included genuine enjoyment in holiday frivolities, I have a casual stance now towards the season. I've scurried through moments of nostalgia, retreated from the province of guilt–*shouldn't I shop, buy gifts for my daughters and their families, even if I don't decorate and bake?* No. I've moved into serenity, far from zones of frenetic activity. Content to read, write, knit, and listen to my own gradually improving piano rendition of Debussy's "Valse Romantique," I'm alone. By choice. And as the 25th approaches, I register my prosperity: how rich I am with my store of memories, and freedom.

Never wedded to traditions, I consciously set about making each Christmas somewhat, or vastly, different from the previous one. I didn't want people to expect things from me, then be disappointed if I couldn't manage to fulfill their hopes. I've extricated myself, however, from the shackles of an old critical bent and don't castigate anyone else for their allegiance to fruitcake, tinsel, Santa or Jesus. I actually admire, sometimes even envy, others for the unwavering energy they put into holiday time and the pleasures they evidently derive from it. And I love looking at their lights! As I sit here gazing out the window, I notice, just across the street, a display so seductive I can't help but be dazzled. Santas, snowmen, reindeer, penguins cavorting, hundreds of colored lights. No nativity, no angels. It's not house-beautiful, but not gaudy, just fun.

As an adolescent, there were two things that thrilled me: Christmas, particularly our tree; and Cincinnati's amusement park, Coney Island. I could hardly wait for Christmas every winter, hardly wait to get to Coney each summer and ride roller coasters, the Wildcat and Shooting Star. As I think about these former passions, I feel a slight twinge of privation. When, how, did I lose the ability to feel grand excitement? It's true, though, occasionally I can still muster up the feeling of *thrill*. Just a little.

I've seen and created some beautiful Christmas trees through the years, but none had the charm of our comparatively modest one on Pine Road, a street aptly named for complementing my reminiscence of the Scotch pines we trimmed with old ornaments my mother had inherited from her grandmother. A golden trumpet, a blue antique auto, red glass swan, angel, Santa hoisting his bag of toys. With the lamps turned off, the living room was a wonder back then. I'd sit on the sofa fingering a bit of stray tinsel, enchanted by bubble lights, and with no understanding of heat and pressure gradient, wonder what magic could make a light so lively. I'd draw close to the tree, bend my face to a big glass ball and delight in seeing myself red or blue or yellow. If only, I felt, shine and color could permanently envelop me.

Our first Christmas in the Pine Road house was enriched, so the grown-ups thought, with an actual appearance of Santa Claus. I was almost four and my mother's sister had just married a few months earlier. Since Aunt Helen had no children yet, she took an interest, I suppose, in witnessing my excitement. Whose idea it was I can't say, but her husband, my Uncle Charles, decided to dress up as Santa and visit our living room.

The German custom of celebrating on Christmas eve instead of morning dictated my mother's approach to paving Santa's way; she put me to bed early, then "woke me up" around 8:00 p.m. after stockings had been stuffed and the jolly old elf had flown off to other chimneys. I emerged from a dark bedroom next to the living room, where I had dutifully stayed waiting for my release, eyes wide open all the while. I don't know if I pretended to wake up, don't know if my mother knew it was impossible to sleep for two early hours of the evening, but none of it mattered when I caught sight of our under-the-tree windfall. This year Santa allowed himself to be seen, resting, presumably, after his strenuous task.

I walked out of the bedroom, looked straight at him and said, "Hi, Uncle Charles!"

Under the fake beard there must have been a crestfallen expression. His vast disappointment became generally known and recounted, and he refused, it was said, to ever come to our house again on Christmas Eve. I teasingly called him Santa Claus for many years.

Without a single memory of how I ascertained that the red-suited man in my living room was not the guy whose belly shook like a bowlful of jelly, I have analyzed my disbelief after studying a photo taken of me that same season with another Santa, at another location. I'm standing by him, instead of sitting in his lap, gazing away from him, with an expression not of fear but perhaps best described as cautious tolerance.

I speculate now that having seen Mr. Claus in one site prior to the holiday, I noticed a distinct enough difference to recognize that Uncle Charles, despite his best attempts to Santa himself, was not the real McNick. And maybe naming him correctly was just good guesswork.

Warm Christmas memories are abundant, but mine are not completely without the blot of sadness. I think of how my mother, divorced in mid-life, frequently alluded to how my father had so often *ruined*, as she termed it, the holiday. She did seem to take pleasure in all the folderol, though she couldn't proclaim it, and mostly grumbled about expenses. When she doled out cookies, there was a smile on her face, and everyone knew she delighted in our praise and happy munching. But that enjoyment was not enough to compensate for my father's drunken harangues after overboard drinking at an office party, or his repeat of the same at the New Year's Eve celebration.

My father's saving grace throughout the season was a certain kind of joviality he had when sober. When he imitated Nat King Cole's "Christmas Song," the old *chestnuts roasting* standby, and got to the words, "he's loaded lots of toys and goodies on his sleigh," he stopped singing after *loaded,* deepening his voice for that word. If she was within earshot, my mother stiffened, and I would note her tight-lipped countenance as the rest of us snickered.

Her dread of my father's uncontrollable, and predictable, drinking, was my mother's legacy to me. As the oldest, most aware of three siblings, I continued to experience throughout my Christmases at home, excitement, but tarnished, like Santa's ashy clothes, by a dark cloud of trepidation.

Tomorrow is Christmas Eve. I'm thinking of going to a candlelight service in the same church my grandmother persuaded my father to attend one year. As an avowed atheist, he had always steadfastly declined to step foot in any church whatsoever. My grandmother was not a church-goer herself (nor was my grandfather), and it was unclear as to whether she had any genuine interest in Christianity. I remember seeing a pamphlet in her house once: the subject was Zoroastrianism. But somehow she had cajoled my father and there we all were, in church, on Christmas Eve. As we were leaving after the service, my grandmother, decked out in her new mink stole, smiled at my father and said, "That was painless, now wasn't it?"

I remember it emerging, his habitual smirk. His reply: "Not exactly."

Will I, atheist that I am, actually go to the candlelight service at that same church I was in, just one time, long ago? I'm not sure. It seems unprincipled, but I do like candles and carols. Seems I'm not content to just sit here on the sofa across from my neighbor's playful penguins and roly-poly Santas, sipping tea and recalling the past; I have to think of principles. And values, customs, power, capitalism, Christianity, and gender. I have to reflect on my disdain for certain aspects of society that enter into my withdrawal from a holiday I once innocently enjoyed. What rankles more, I muse, the general dictates of buying or worshipping? Or the universal acceptance that women, for the most part only women, will shop, wrap, bake, roast, and decorate away their time and energy to make Christmas fit the parameters that have been set for it? (Oh, I know, many just love doing it!) Into my reminiscing, these considerations creep. How did it come to be prescribed that everyone should trim a chopped-down tree and shop till they drop? Buy, buy, buy, you who are unduly affected by, and oblivious to, the greed factor of American dreaming.

I suppose I won't go to that candlelight service tonight. I'll stay here in this small house, and if I allow myself to be drawn further into memory-land, I might listen to the strains of "White Christmas," "Silver Bells," "Santa Baby," and the like. With a modicum of effort, I think I can block any surge of sentiment through my renegade self.

It has arrived, the 25th. I'm looking at the pile of laundry next to my desk where I write. I think I'll throw a load into the washer. Might as well go to the local Starbuck's now–yes, it's open—and check my email. I have no internet connection in this writer's retreat, since I'm unwilling to pay for it here. Will the Starbuck's cashier wish me a merry Christmas, as everyone was doing all week, everywhere I went? Interesting how we never seem to use the word *merry* anymore except for Christmas-wishing. It hasn't morphed, however, into something altogether different, like *gay*.

This is not the place to check email, after all. Unexpectedly crowded, the shop has a line going out the door, and even if I were patient enough to wait my turn to place an order, it's likely there would be no available seat then. It's eleven a.m. Why aren't these people home playing with their kids' Christmas toys?

Suddenly, I remember a recent visit to the library where I overheard a librarian tell someone you could access the internet from the parking lot. Around the corner from Starbuck's, the library's closed, the parking lot empty. I pull into a space, turn the car off and the laptop on. It works; I'm online. A few messages. I answer them, then drive home.

My clothes are clean. I put them in the dryer. Next, I do the things I always do: read, write, knit, practice piano, etc. I go walk in the park, then evening arrives. It's Sunday; as usual, I watch *60 Minutes* on TV.

So this is what it's like to do nothing special, go nowhere, see no one, neither bake nor eat a single holiday treat, accept no invitations, exchange no gifts, sit in a living room on Pine Road with no lights winking out from a lovingly decorated tree. I have satisfied my desire to see what it would be like to have extreme deliverance from the holiday. So how do I feel?

Indifferent. Purely indifferent? No, my feelings are seldom pure. But there's a way I have trained my brain to keep certain thoughts and memories high in my head, not allowing them to sink lower, closer to my eyes, my heart. They also cannot stay long, even in the upper region; I quickly whisk them away, not giving them the opportunity to occupy my entire being, vandalize my prized serenity. I like, however, the challenge of seeing just how much I can explore old memories without experiencing that type of invasion.

I'm thinking now of a faraway Christmas. Still married, I was persuaded by my husband to find a country inn where we could spend Christmas. He liked retreats away from others, but with his family. Our daughters, aged fifteen and seven, were agreeable to the idea of leaving our New Jersey home and hopping over to Connecticut to a country inn. We loaded the car with wrapped gifts and set out.

Once in the quaint village, we easily found the inn, whose decor and furnishings, we saw, were not quite shabby but not exactly snappy. But there we were for a week, and it was just good enough. We were in a festive mood and would not be persuaded to be anything but jolly. Even I, who had to settle in with a bundle of freshman comp papers. Since I was teaching at a college for the first time, I was an ingénue, without a clue as to how arduous the grading detail could be. I was actually looking forward to reading the papers and placing the A-B-C-D's–in this pre-computer time–in a little grade book. It was to be the last time, this first time, that I would *happily* anticipate the task.

When I was not reading compositions, I hung out with the family, playing cards and games, taking turns with my daughter playing Christmas carols on the piano in the lounge. There were almost no other guests at the inn, so much of the time we were free to do as we liked, without the worry of disturbing anyone. We went for walks through the snowy streets and took photos of ourselves in our new winter coats. We enjoyed the food at the inn, though it was mostly uninspired. On Christmas Eve we did go to a candlelight service in a tiny chapel we had come upon. And that's about all I remember of our country inn holiday.

My clothes are dry. I toss them on the bed for folding later and settle on the sofa with *The School of Essential Ingredients*, a book that a friend had given me. All is silent and calm here on Pine Road, my old home ground, in a house devoid of tree, tinsel, angel, and stockings.

DETACHED, UNRAVELING, DISMISSED, AND AFTERMATH

Newspaper editor; captain of the Wildcatettes; secretary of student council; Most Outstanding English student; kickline dancer, albeit undistinguished, in the annual variety show. The all-American applecart I traveled in during high school should have led me, smoothly, straight into adulthood, and some kind of success. Instead...it tipped over; I fell out.

Contributing to the upset was my failure to become a cheerleader. And I don't mean the failure per se, and resulting disappointment, which was real then, but, rather, what that failure represented: an inability to sincerely cheer a bunch of boys running, kicking and throwing around their balls, an insincerity that must have shone through my less-than-lively attempts to simulate cheering when I tried out for the squad. I thought I wanted to be the cheering sort, since they were much admired, so I tried to fabricate pep even when it was evident I had little. The judges were not fooled.

I finally understood, when I was riding in the back of a station wagon with my cheerleader friends after a football game, that I would never fit into the pack. Our school's team had lost, and the girls were crying. Incredulous, I was sure they were playacting. But real tears wet their cheeks, and why, I wondered? They hadn't lost the game; their jumps were high; their calls, loud; their pep, enlivening. And their wish for a win was fervent. Anyway, whatever possible cheering deficiency they might have had could not have affected the outcome of the game, which was, after all, just a game, so why cry for a loss that was the boys' doing? But I was alone in my thinking, I knew, understanding that those who cheered could cry as well. Still, I distrusted that their mournfulness was authentic, and if my efforts during cheerleader tryouts had been spiritless, their weeping over *our* defeat was, in my view, something akin to crocodile tears. Suspicious, yes. I knew I was following in my cynic-father's footsteps.

It's a commonplace understanding that we all want to be loved, and I had wanted my father, first Richard in my life, to love me. Then I wanted some boy to love me. That is, until one did, my second Richard. Strawberry blonde and green-eyed, cleft in chin, dimple in right cheek, over six feet tall and every micron imbued with Old Spice and spearmint gum, he was irresistible. So-o-o sexy, but in a loving, wholesome way. I can't capture in words the rapture, but rapture it was. For awhile. Until he became too devoted. Until I realized that his beautiful packaging did not come with many well-developed mental parts. Then, too, I started to view myself as someone who would not, could not, stay with one person and so began the disengagement, very long, slow, and painful, despite being of my own making.

    I did love Dick. Never have I known anyone quite so devoted, so flirtatious (with me only, it seemed), so loving, so sexy, anyone who exuded such sweetness as he did (but the first-love aspect of our relationship must have something to do with a years-later appraisal). For almost six years I loved him, through high school and into my second year of college. We didn't *go steady*, commonly done at that time, since my mother forbid it, and I opposed it, but we were intensely connected. He taught me to drive, bought me embroidered and lace blouses, White Shoulders perfume, a pearl ring. Winter nights we ice-skated on Sharon Woods Lake, water-skied in summer on the Ohio River behind the boat he and his friend Daryl had bought together. Parking on lonely roads at night, we struggled—me to preserve my virginity (a *must* at the time), he to sabotage it. When we drove home, the car radio was always on, lyrics clear and angst-ridden, or mawkish to my fast-jading ears. They seemed to spell out much of our drama: "One Summer Night"; "I Love How You Love Me"; "Mr. Blue." I'm like Mr. Blue, Dick would tell me, our years together scarred with breakups all initiated by me, like the song says,

> Our guardian star lost all his glow
> The day that I lost you
> He lost all his glitter the day you said no
> And his silver turned to blue...

In our off-times, Catholic Dick dated two good Catholic girls who adored him (appropriate girls, unlike the budding atheist I was). Maggie was the kind of girl who would set his mother's hair for her, a helpfulness that wouldn't have occurred to me. Pauline, perky, blonde and beautiful, was captain of her cheerleader squad at a Catholic high school. I saw them together once, Dick and Pauline; they made a striking couple. So whenever I was on the verge of ending our affair, I'd tell him he'd be better off with Maggie or Pauline.

Following a breakup, I'm not sure which I liked more: the power I felt when, upon my beckoning, he quickly returned, or the exquisite experience of making up. One evening in the fall after we had been apart for a month (the maximum duration of our separations), he arrived at my house in his blue Chevy, dressed in his blue sweater, redolent, as always, of the Old Spice-spearmint combo. As he walked up the sidewalk to my front porch where I waited, trying to appear nonchalant, he smiled. His post-breakup smile was always slightly sheepish, as though he had been the one at fault, the one who had insisted we were through. We got in his car and went to visit his friend Dennis, who was going to get married within the month. Dick was to be the best man. When we arrived at Dennis' house and parked, we lingered, neither of us ready to step out of our renewed intimacy. I think if those few moments, kissing in his car, had somehow been corporified, they surely would have been peaches, perfectly ripe, sweet and round.

After visiting the groom-to-be, Dick had marriage on his mind, and the evening's ecstatic charge, like a battery, went dead. What am I doing with him, I thought later, after he had dropped me at home. It's all wrong; it can't last, but why, why can't I stay away from him?

A problem that wouldn't resolve: Dick couldn't read. At least not very well. So I'd try to tutor him.

"You have to study," I'd lecture.

"I want to, " his reply, "for you."

I was enraged. "No! You have to want it for yourself!"

"I do, but I want to do it for you, too," he would hold my hand, looking earnest. And pretty soon I'd break up with him again.

There was no question of a happily-ever-after, but we went on and on, until Dick dropped out of high school, and I went off to college. Our final break-up, wrenching, took place on the Miami University campus when Dick had come to visit me during my sophomore year. It was a cowardly and poorly executed affair that I tried to pull off by sneaking out of an uptown bar and leaving him sitting there alone as I walked back to my dorm. But in the morning his car was on the street, and he was slumped down in the front seat where he had spent the night.

I had to face him after all and climbed into the car to sit next to him. He cried, and then I did, too. It was over. A comment from my high school English teacher Mr. Spencer, when friends and I visited him long after graduation, was telling: "Jim [another of my English teachers] and I always wondered why the smartest girl in the school was dating the dumbest boy." Overstated at both extremes, perhaps, but encapsulating. And I wouldn't be quite honest if I didn't say I was pleased with at least part of the assessment.

I was not the cowboy I had fantasized being when I was a little girl. I was not devoted to Dick, didn't want to be married, had dismissed the idea of being a fashion designer or illustrator after years of drawing and sharing creations with my friend Janiece and our California friend Sharon who had moved away at the end of fourth grade. We had been sending our latest fashions back and forth throughout middle school and into high school, and I was convinced for a long time that the three of us would enter the world of fashion as soon as we graduated from college. I had even chosen a name for myself: *Lenora Reed*. Then came the time when I gave it all up, after my first, and only, college art class. I had concluded that fashion was inconsequential, and at the same time hated having someone tell me how to draw. The industry, too—though I can't imagine how I had arrived at my conviction—was probably dominated and controlled by men.

Having come to terms with the immutable fact of my female gender, I still chafed at all feminine stereotypes. Nor did I care about fulfilling expectations. I'll remain unmarried, I thought, but will not consider the typical careers for women: secretary, teacher, nurse, librarian. However, when I reflected on the dictionary explanation of *spinster*, I was appalled: "In modern everyday English, spinster cannot be used to mean simply 'unmarried woman'; as such, it is a derogatory term, referring or alluding to a stereotype of an older woman who is unmarried, childless, prissy, and repressed."

It was common knowledge that *bachelor* was never a derogatory term, and that such a man was often envied, his unmarried state implying freedom, especially freedom to form as many transitory romantic/sexual connections he wanted, without incrimination. Well, gender be damned, I'd just call myself a bachelor then, knowing the world would not agree, feeling more and more detached from this strange place *world*, where I moved so uneasily.

Junior year in high school. I'm overtaken by listlessness and a mindset increasingly critical of everything and everyone. I don't know why. I wonder who I am and how I got this way. Less and less satisfied with the things I'm doing, uninterested in my studies, I fail algebra, which I'm actually good at; then, jolted by the F, I rise, phoenix-wise, to a new but temporary cloud of caring.

On my subsequent report card, *A* sits next to loathsome *F*, accompanied by the teacher's note: "Shows what could have been accomplished had she applied herself throughout the year." Looming always in the background is the specter of parental repercussions, expectations of academic success real, though largely unspoken.

How can I apply myself, I wonder, when nothing seems to matter? And yet...complete withdrawal from things would condemn me to an outsider's status and censure, for which I still have a horror. I'm an impostor, I keep thinking, in each sphere where I'm lodged: student milieu, governing, entertaining, reporting. *Oh, yes, I'm the great pretender*, sing the Platters, and those words reverberate within me.

Senior year. I forgo participation in the variety show that I had always loved but have come to see as trivial. I refuse to go on the Washington, D.C. trip, knowing that close conjunction with a group of students and chaperones would be taxing. Nor do I want to ask my mother for the necessary travel money, only to hear her usual lecture on how tight money is.

I discover T.S. Eliot and read, over and over, in bed at night "The Hollow Men":

> Our dried voices, when
> We whisper together
> Are quiet and meaningless
> As wind in dry grass
> Or rats' feet over broken glass
> In our dry cellar.

Just that meaningless, all words, I think, though my accordance is curious, and I become obsessed with figuring myself out. I know I'm enamored of Eliot, his poetry, the idea of writing poems. Lines from "Preludes" lodge in me: "the burnt-out ends of smoky days"; "withered leaves about your feet"; "one thinks of all the hands/that are raising dingy shades/in a thousand furnished rooms"; "some infinitely gentle/infinitely suffering thing." I think I am this *suffering thing*, though my suffering is indistinct, indecipherable. I know neither its origin nor significance.

My English teacher Mr. Spencer assigns us the task of writing a sonnet, and I write "Inquiries of Death":

> Can death be beautiful as some have said,
> A kingdom being not of lords and slaves,
> But everlasting happiness instead,
> Invites, beckons, lures us to our graves.
> And yet I have heard such appalling tales
> Of life's cessation; the gates of torment
> Open wide, and never-ending peace fails
> To greet us. Will nature never relent?
> I only ask, "Is death so glorious,
> Or is it filled with agony? Will sin
> Prevail and speak in tones obstreperous,
> Or shall the world see love and honor win?"
> To these queries have I heard but lies,
> For the mystery lives with he who dies.

I'm told my sonnet is the best one in the class: "excellent" though it "stretches rhythm at times," my teacher's written comments. I mark this bit of writing as the start of my idèe fixe: death.

Through senior year I resist, somewhat, my opposing sardonic self, continue my leadership enterprises, easy enough to carry on with a modicum of genuine interest. In the end, though, I'm not cut out for any of those activities, and I realize that without the wherewithal to assess just who I am, I simply do them because they confer recognition and approval. I remain semi-attached to boyfriend Dick who seems to love me unwaveringly.

I love that he loves me.

Freshman year at the university. When I arrive, I'm in awe of myself, wide-eyed and disbelieving. Me, on a college campus? It's thrilling, but I'm immediately stunned by those freshmen who seem so confident, so comfortable in their new surroundings. I'm not. Then my high school friend, Janiece, persuades me to go through the week of sorority rush with her, but as we proceed I can't help question: how can you go to a 15-minute party, a 30-minute party, then an hour party ten times and decide which sorority has girls you want as "sisters"? How am I going to connect with these stranger-sisters? Nonetheless, soon enough I'm a *pledge*, subject to hell-week, assigned a *big sister* to guide me along the path to *going active*. Active I go, pay dues, buy the rubied and pearled pin, attend meetings; a year later I drop out, Holden Caulfield's female counterpart, fixated on *phoniness*.

My college campus is defined by sorority/fraternity life and without the Greek stamp on your chest you're consigned to nonentity-land, whose population seems sparse. I make my lonely way, then, during sophomore year, finding a casual friend here and there but becoming more and more solitary. I'm thoroughly self-absorbed, detached and increasingly aloof from Janiece, who fits in, bonding with the inmates in our female prison-dorm and, true to form, continues in her role as most popular girl. Inwardly scornful of squeals down the hall when a boy calls or comes to visit, I can't seem to adapt to plaid skirt and knee sock uniformity. I rail against the girl-dorm, boy-dorm division where boys have no rules about the hours they keep and girls must be in the locked dorm by 10:00 pm during the week, midnight on Saturdays. I have no sea legs in this sea of girls who flirt and back-bite with a virtuosity I don't have. Except for an occasional faint twinge, though, I never mind being a misfit; considering my life from backyard internment through school and into college, a certain measure of misfittery is so familiar I'm hardly troubled by the condition.

Solipsism: self is the only reality; egoistic self-absorption. I'm happy to learn this word, and wear its contours like a coat, idiosyncratic and warm. High-visibility and popularity have come to seem like a fast road to the same meaninglessness anonymity furnishes. I think I like being a nobody and don't analyze this transformation or consider how it has come to be. It just feels right. It would be many years before I'd come upon the Emily Dickinson poem that begins:

> I'm Nobody! Who are you?
> Are you–Nobody–too?

One day my geology professor informs our class that if a standard-length movie were made about life on planet Earth, the human would appear in about the last two minutes. For me, his comment is not just interesting, but shocking, then illuminating. In a flash, I comprehend what has been contributing to my ennui: some kind of insight about human significance, which is, in fact, insignificance. No longer is my growing withdrawal from the world baffling.

Sartre's *Nausea,* which I read instead of studying, nurtures my self-alienation:

> I live alone, entirely alone. I never speak to anyone, never... Now when I say "I," it seems hollow to me... It would be better if I could only stop thinking.... Nothing happens while you live. The scenery changes, people come in and go out, that's all. There are no beginnings. Days are tacked on to days without rhyme or reason, an interminable, monotonous addition.

I don't want a string of monotonous days, in a stretch of life whose length is unpredictable, whose death is inescapable. What's the point, I ask myself. I don't want it, no, I don't want it. Life. Or love.

At night I walk the streets behind my dormitory, night after night, through the spring of 1964, darkness, solitude, and movement somehow soothing. I don't study, barely socialize, simply wallow in my languor, which is, strangely, a kind of ecstasy. I could just die now. Why not? Yes, cut it short, this existence I never requested, could not have requested or refused, *existence*, which for an atheist-existentialist like me is ludicrous. Keats' "Ode to a Nightingale":

> Darkling I listen; and, for many a time
>   I have been half in love with easeful Death,
> Call'd him soft names in many a mused rhyme,
>   To take into the air my quiet breath;
> Now more than ever seems it rich to die,
>   To cease upon the midnight with no pain....

Somewhere along the way, I fall half in love with death myself, and my passion for it eclipses all other ardor. Age twenty and I'm thinking I may be done with life, so notwithstanding a lack of savvy about the best ways to die, I plot my quietus.

On a Friday night in May, I finish reading Joseph Conrad's *Victory,* from which five short passages are the first entries in my small notebook of quotes, each echoing a thought/feeling I had been having. Most germane: "At one time I thought that intelligent observation of facts was the best way of cheating the time which is allotted to us whether we want it or not, but now I have done with observation, too."

Three semesters of college had me in observation mode and like Conrad's Axel Heyst, I was done. I had seen so little, but I knew, instinctively, the world was not a place for me, existence was not a state in which to continue.

I set Conrad on my desk and go downstairs to the dorm's rec room, watch an old war-time movie on TV, *Love Is a Many Splendored Thing,* and when it's over I return to my room. In accordance with the plan and timetable (my roommate has left for the weekend), I sit on the bed with a bottle and a glass of water. Methodically, I swallow little yellow pills, one after another…

Dependent on counseling during the last two weeks of school, permission is granted for me to take final exams and get credit for my spring courses. But I can't return to the university in the fall; I'm expelled. Already feeling the sharp points of failure, an outcome I had never considered when I planned the ending of my insignificant life, I'm further mortified by the expulsion.

We sit and stare at each other, the university psychologist and I, the student mandated to meet with him. Crisp and severe-looking with his wire-rimmed glasses and close-cropped salt-and-pepper hair, he's the same at each of three requisite sessions: silent and staring. He doesn't speak, waiting, I suppose, for me to talk. But I have nothing to say, nothing. Not to him or anyone else.

This may not be a work of art and it will have very little literary value; but there is one thing certain-----the main issue will not be cleverly disguised. No digging or hunting. It will be completely understandable. That is, understandable to the degree that you will know exactly what I am saying, although you may not understand <u>why</u> I am saying it. Although I will try to make the <u>why</u> as clear as possible. This is written, rather than stated verbally, for just one reason. I do not feel that I am capable of talking to you unemotionally.

This was the start of my father's letter to me, typed while I was in the same room with him. I was twenty-one and had just spent the year running wild after my dismissal from the university. The letter went on, detailing my unacceptable post-college life, which included carousing and late nights, until he eventually got to the meat of his vexation:

> *Ever since your little suicide attempt, my life has changed. Hardly a day passes without remembering that moment when I was informed of what had happened. I will never be able to forget that ride to Oxford* [Ohio]. *I keep asking why, why, why? Was it the school work—were you trying so hard to make us proud of you and couldn't make the grades? Was it the broken love affair? Was it because you weren't popular? Or were you? Because you didn't have enough money? Or the combination of all these? Or was it because your father drank! Because maybe once a year he came home stupid? Was it because your mother was too strict? You never did explain.*

He was disturbed, too, by the fact that I hadn't left a note, but I had thought only people who were attempting suicide as a cry for help wrote notes. Since I was not one of those, I hadn't bothered to write one. And none of his speculation included the truth. No, not grades, broken love affair, popularity, money, or his drinking. Conclusions I had made about human existence were simplistic but compelling: it was pointless; always carried the possibility of pain, physical and/or psychic; it eventually ended. These certitudes, as I viewed them, prompted a desire to terminate my meaningless existence. Why wait and endure, was my thinking, for an inevitable end. But I didn't want to attempt to explain myself, at the risk of being belittled.

I can't remember a single thing about my reaction to my father's letter, which so clearly demonstrated his feelings when he was compelled to write it: frustration, anger, sorrow, perplexity, love. I don't know if I cried when I read it, don't know if I *tried* to explain myself. I ponder and wonder if I was so profoundly affected by the letter that I suppressed all memory of our subsequent interaction. Maybe. I can't say with any certainty. The letter, however, is real: paper yellowed but the black words from an ink ribbon still well-defined, many underlined, mistakes X'd out, evidence of the emotional speed with which he had banged it out on the typewriter, two pages single-spaced. No heading, no date, no greeting, no signature. And my mother said nothing to me at all, a fact I never registered through the years until I came to this page where I would write something about the aftermath of my failed suicide attempt. So removed from each other were we that it didn't even seem strange–until now–that she had no questions, no comments.

I lived with my parents that summer of 1964 and went to a boring job each day at an insurance company. Setting up medical claims for an examiner to review and pay, I had a desk with a never-dwindling stack of doctors' reports from which I hand-copied diagnoses onto the company's claim forms as quickly and efficiently as could be done in those pre-computer days. The best that can be said about the job is that I learned lovely words and phrases, like *arteriosclerosis, cardiopulmonary, leukemia, myocardial infarction.*

In preparation for this particular job, I had to spend two weeks in the files learning what happened before the claim business progressed to my desk. The shelves, almost floor to ceiling, were suffocatingly close to each other, and the young women who pulled and re-filed manila folders nine-to-five seemed to disavow how deplorable the work was.

"How do you like the job," one woman asked after my first week.

"I hate it," I answered bluntly, going on to say something, I'm sure, about just how bad a job it was. The supervisor got wind of my minor dissidence, which to her was major.

"Don't say anything negative about the filing!" Julie cautioned. "These girls don't know it's a bad job, and that's the way we want to keep it."

I wasn't at all convinced that the file clerks were so unwitting, but, despite my conviction that they knew the work was absolutely low-end, I kept quiet.

To mitigate the noxious nine-to-five monotony of my days, I read at lunch time and nighttime the writers relevant for me. Sylvia Plath became the most important when in July I found an American poetry anthology in the library that contained a couple of her poems, a photo and bio of her, including the significant detail of her suicide just the year before. I had been unacquainted with her work, her life, her death. So I'm not alone in wanting to hasten my unavoidable death, I thought..., but I had failed and reconsidered, whereas she was gone. My decision to keep living had been an easy choice, the humiliation of a possible second suicide failure untenable.

Years have passed since I discovered Plath, and as I review my life and write of my limited engagement with it, I think of my Plath collection, which includes first editions of her poetry books and every biography ever written about her. It's as though the strings of words have served as silken cords to keep me bound to earth and existence. And it's as though a certain *me* did die in 1964, a new one reappearing. I never contemplated suicide again, though my conviction that living is pointless forms the backbone of my continuing existence.

In response to Plath's "Lady Lazarus" ("Dying/is an art, like everything else./I do it exceptionally well") and "Edge" ("The woman is perfected/Her dead/Body wears the smile of accomplishment"), I wrote:

> Alive, a woman is perfected. In a hood of bone
> She's equal to the staring.
> Dying's not an art, it's a consequence;
> It's living that needs a gifted hand.

Along with my Plath collection, I still have my notebook of quotes begun in 1964 and maintained to 1986. If it exists, I exist...though this may be a weird bit of logic.

By the end of summer, my supervisor Julie and I had bonded, and I became her roommate in an efficiency apartment, actually the basement of an old house. We shared the rent: $50 a month. There was a bed at one end of the room, a couch and coffee table in the middle, and the front end had a bar with a refrigerator, sink, and stove behind it. A small bathroom was off to the side. Soon we added a third-floor room to our arrangement for an extra monthly $10 and put a mattress on the floor, a poster of Greenwich Village, where I longed to live, on the wall. The space was meant to be a retreat for reading and writing but with working by day, playing at night, not much of either was accomplished.

It was a heady time for me though, cut loose from my mother's apron-string suppression; I reveled in my freedom. Days at the insurance company were tolerable because of the nights that followed, hanging out with Julie at places called Babe's, the Nebisch, the Mug Club, where we could dance and meet up with guys.

Despite Julie's frequent mention of Tim, a boyfriend who was in the service, she was always ready to flirt and drink and rendezvous with this guy and that who crossed her path. I questioned her allegiance to Tim, a name she pronounced "Tee-im," with her charming Kentucky accent.

"He's the one I'm going to marry," she insisted.

"Are you sure?" I raised my eyebrows. Not having met him, I couldn't imagine that this fun-loving roommate of mine could be devoted to someone she hadn't seen in months. Julie would smile and nod. And then...

"C'mon! Let's go," she'd say and we'd be off to the bars, drinking having become our favorite pastime.

Hanging out at Babe's one night, Julie and I were dancing together like so many girls did until they linked up with a guy. After awhile, we sat down to rest and were sipping Harvey Wall-bangers when a guy came to our table and asked me to dance. One look at him and I realized he was someone I knew from the past, though he evidently didn't recognize me at first. We had dated for a month or so during my sophomore year in high school. This was my Dave Number One and turned out to be my Sexual Experience Number Two, after high school Dick. Dave loved to have sex in a barn and knew a good one we could sneak into. Not as captivated by straw as he was, nonetheless, I braved it a couple of times. By the end of summer, sensing he was proving to be a bit more serious than I had bargained for, I hid from him in the restroom of a bar where he had come looking for me. Déjà vu! I remembered hiding from high school boyfriend Dick. What a ridiculous tactic, which never seemed to work!

"Why did you throw me over for the bars?" Dave asked the next day when he called. "I was going to ask you to marry me!"

I didn't say *I know*, can't remember what reason I gave. In any case, that was the end of Dave One.

Julie's Tee-im came home, and sure enough, she married him. So I moved to another place, and then another, and another...each time having a reason for my relocation. For seven months I stayed at my insurance job, writing cardio and lympho-type words, day in, day out, all the way to burnout, trying to feel, really feel, my freedom. As Erich Maria Remarque wrote, "Only when one had nothing more to live for, was one free." I had nothing to live for, and no ambition to die.

I began to scan newspaper want ads, looking for another job, and finally answered one placed by another insurance company. Management there was looking for a woman aged twenty-five to forty to be an underwriter-trainee, but I, just twenty-one, called anyway. When I talked to the HR man, I was forced at last to reveal my age, then told thanks-but-no-thanks (age discrimination on the young end of the continuum). It so happened, though, that Julie was working for an employment agency housed in an office one floor above the insurance company, and, enterprising and assertive that she was, managed to get an appointment for me with the same HR man who had rejected me over the phone.

The interview seemed to go well, and this guy didn't know I was the would-be applicant he had talked to already and refused to see. Eventually he noticed my date of birth on the employment application, however, and began to explain the age requirement...then,

"Oh, well, since you're already here," he interrupted himself, "you might as well go ahead and take the tests. If you want to."

"Tests?"

"Yeah, just verbal and math stuff––to make sure you can read, add, subtract," he smiled.

"Okay," I agreed, then wound up spending all morning on a bunch of timed tests. When I finished, I was told they'd let me know the outcome, and I left, taking my too-young-self home with little hope of getting the job.

Late that afternoon–hired! The man who had conducted the interview called to tell me.

"Your scores were higher than anyone else's, anyone I've ever interviewed," he said. "Can you come in Monday about 8:30?"

I transported from Insurance Company One to Two a few books that had been loaned to me by a guy named John whom I usually ate lunch with. I called him to see when and where I could return his books, and he suggested having a drink after work. I agreed and he picked me up at 5:30 since I didn't own a car, and soon we entered a playful state in The Playpen, a bar John knew of. *A* drink turned out to be a *surfeit* as the hour grew later and later, culminating in a confession of mutual attraction, a declaration that we both believed in free love, and, finally, a plan to run away together. To Spain. John had pulled out a magazine to show me an article about cheap living there for writers, and we were both aspiring writers, so why not go?

As we drank to each other and our proposition, celebrating what was definitely a half-assed scheme, we discussed our major stumbling block: his wife.

"I'm just gonna tell her."

"Are you sure?"

"Hey, we haven't been getting along that well anyway," John insisted. "I've been thinking of leaving and finding my own place."

"But couldn't free love include staying married?" I was beginning to doubt my comfort level with a home-wrecker label. At least they didn't have kids; is the wrecking of a childless home less heinous, I wondered.

"She's not really interested in doing anything outside marriage. So she sure won't want to stick with me if she knows someone else is in the picture."

The upshot was that John went home at 3:00 a.m. and woke his wife *Jackie* to say he was leaving her for *Jacqui*. Yes, we had the same name, albeit different spellings. After his announcement, he slept for a few hours, got up, found an apartment, and began moving in. Now, I was young, but not unaware that when men say they're going to leave their wives they postpone it, often indefinitely, or else flat out never accomplish it, often never intend to, so I was nonplussed at this fait accompli. Oh, well, I thought, the life I hadn't wanted was certainly rife with interesting developments.

My time with John was fun: reading and writing poetry together; playing his Joan Baez records; driving around town in his little red Triumph convertible; barhopping. We frequented Herbie's, a place he introduced me to, where on a Friday night we could listen to jazz performed by a quartet, and when they took a break, a solo pianist. Certain piano songs became my favorites "Satin Doll," "My Delight," and "Green Dolphin Street," and I couldn't help but register that the guy on the keyboard was talented, young, black, and cute.

I had begun to formulate my justification for living by this time, which drew upon the adage "living well is the best revenge." Whom I was avenging and what living well actually meant, I couldn't say. But however I came to have my unsolicited existence, aside from an act of copulation, I figured *he/she/it* would be repaid for the affront if I could go on living just as I was doing with John, the essence of it *carefree*.

Meanwhile, I was happy working at the insurance company whose office was in the Carew Tower, Cincinnati's tallest building at the time. I liked the job, liked working with all men, as the company's test case in female underwriting, and enjoyed roaming the arcade at lunch time.

Most of all, I savored my superiority, a delusion, to be sure. Haughtily, and foolishly, I held myself above those women who formed the secretarial pool.

One day at lunchtime when I was in the employment lounge eating and reading the paper, I saw an article reporting the death of T. S. Eliot.

"Oh! Eliot died!" I blurted out.

One of the secretaries said, "What?!" Soon everyone at the table was talking about what would happen next on the show. I had no idea what they were referring to since I had never seen this show, of which they were all clearly in the know, even besotted, you might say. They assumed the Eliot I had mentioned was *Elliot Carson*, a character on...*Peyton Place*. Though I had read the book, precisely because my mother told me not to, I had never seen the TV program; in those days I didn't own a television, had never thought of buying one. When would I watch it? I had to work all day and my carousing time at night was sacrosanct. And I preferred to live a soap opera, rather than watch one. Finally, I murmured the truth, that the dead Eliot was not theirs. Fish out of water, the secretarial pool, I was similarly set apart from the land of underwriters and would later grasp the reality of that.

The current episode of my own soap opera soon had a denouement as my affair with John ended before we could get to Spain. I had gone out one night, spontaneously, with a male co-worker to have dinner, and when John tried to call me (long before cell phones facilitated timely communication) and couldn't reach me, he seemed to degenerate into a lapsed believer in free love.

Although no love, free or otherwise, had been made before, during, or after my dinner, I had to listen to a healthy measure of vitriol as John berated me for–though he didn't name it–my infidelity. I concluded that dinner, not to mention love or sex, with the opposite gender, was to be enjoyed *freely* by men, not women. John was not simply a lapsed believer but a full-blown hypocrite, as possessive as any other man on the street. He soon went back to his wife, and I went on my slightly-less-than-merry way, for a brief (very brief!) time. I never saw John again.

Not one to dawdle when it came to the prospect of a new quest, I convinced myself that I wanted to go to that jazz bar Herbie's to hear jazz, accompanied or not by the likes of a John. So I went alone, sat right at the bar, and from there my next drama began to unfold. Of course, I knew that as much as I loved the music, I had an ulterior motive, knew it but would not have admitted it to anyone.

Maybe I did seem a bit forlorn when he asked me why I looked so sad. The *he* was Harvey, the pianist who sat down next to me after playing "Satin Doll."

"Where's your boyfriend?"

"He's not my boyfriend anymore." Was I or was I not feeling sad about it?

"Oh?" his smile was dazzling.

"Yeah," I said, "it's over."

And suddenly I was euphoric to be saying that!

I don't recall how I managed to convey that I had taken a bus to get to Herbie's, but I did, and Harvey drove me home that night, home being a nice little apartment I had found after Julie married and moved on, my first unshared living space ever.

I began seeing a lot of Harvey, going with him when he had various gigs in both Ohio and Indiana bars, meeting his mother and two sisters, spending time at his house, learning how to smoke marijuana. Very quickly, I decided that my apartment was not a convenient location for my office and the bars and parks I most liked. I had always wanted to live in the area that I thought approximated New York's Greenwich Village, a Cincinnati hilltop neighborhood called Mt. Adams, formerly Mt. Ida. A note on the original name: Ida had been a washerwoman who lived in the hollow of a sycamore tree on a hill, but, when the Cincinnati Observatory opened in 1843, housing the most powerful telescope of its kind, the mount was renamed, after John Quincy Adams, who delivered a dedication address for the observatory. Naturally, the choice between washerwoman and president was a clear one. Entrenched anyway, the practice of naming places after men, almost never women. What Cincinnatians even knew that the city's bohemian haven was once called Mt. Ida?

Home to the Art Museum and Playhouse in the Park, Mt. Adams seemed to be open to art, music...and diversity. So once again I took up a newspaper to look for apartment rentals. Still without a car, I made my way to places by bus and on foot, finally finding an off-the-beaten-Mt. Adams-path address, affordable and available. I was completely charmed by the fact that a few paces down the street there was a visible handrail that followed what seemed like a downhill million steps that went straight out onto Fifth Street, which for half a mile or so led right to the Carew Tower where I worked.

With Harvey, a good job, and a Mt. Adams apartment, my program of living well continued: restitution at its finest, I thought.

DETERMINATION

Was it because.... You never did explain, my father wrote in his letter, going on to detail other unfathomable things about me.

> *Until that day, I would have bet my life on you. As a girl who really knew what she wanted out of life and sharp enough to probably get it. I still believe this, but I'll be damned if I know what you want. What has happened? There was a time when you couldn't tolerate "hicks," as you called them, and then you chose to <u>live</u> with Julie! Now don't champion her. Because she isn't in your class in any way whatsoever. She is a grade A Briar.*

Class. My class. What is it, I thought to myself, what constitutes class? Is someone relegated to a particular class by virtue of where they were born and to whom? Is it like caste then, something you can never exit, something created by whatever human despots? [And now, so many years later, I've come upon, bought, and read *Caste* by Isabel Wilkerson, "a reexamination of what lies under the surface of American life today"–pervasive racism.] I do think my father was deeply concerned with class, though I hadn't yet put together a picture of him as someone disturbed by his own seemingly middle one, someone who maybe longed for a higher status.

Julie was from Kentucky, and in 1965 that was a strike against her in my father's view. Yes, we had all, in my Cincinnati family, made derogatory comments about people from across the river, lumping them together in a pack we called, variously, *hicks, briars, hillbillies*. And that *pack* was closely aligned with what I concluded must be *class*. We had no close associations with anyone who could possibly belong to these undesirable assemblies. I had been indoctrinated by my father, but only partially, it seemed, so when I met Julie I didn't characterize her as a "grade A Briar." Despite early influences, my inclination was to individually assess those who crossed my path. I liked Julie; we connected; I moved in with her. Period. She was smart, friendly, outgoing, pretty, engaging. I didn't interview her or ask for a pedigree, I just embraced her. She didn't have a college degree, but so what? Neither did I. We lived together for a few months, harmoniously, and I hold fond memories of our escapades.

Although I remember no conversation with my father about the concerns he laid out in the letter, we must have had one, of sorts, my father arguing with a protest he said I made:

> *Your statement the other night really floored me. "You never have approved of anyone I've brought around"----or words to that effect.*

He countered with his reasonable objections to two boyfriends, then got to the *raison d'être* for his short catalogue of undesirable boyfriends, justifying his disapproval of the final one on the list:

> *(3) The present friend whom you are "dating"-- my disapproval is not entirely because he is a negro----but chiefly because you undoubtedly went out of your way to find him. May I explain-----had you met a colored boy at college in one of your classes or accidentally in your work and it gradually grew into a warm friendship filled with understanding, I would probably have had to accept it- as prejudiced as I am. But this affair obviously did not come about in this manner.*

Numerous and various, our opportunities for misunderstanding. No, I had not met Harvey in a college classroom. But class intermingled with race in my father's evaluations and assumptions: if Harvey had been, the implication, a college student, he would have been nearing the status of acceptable, despite his race. Well, Harvey, unlike me, was a <u>college graduate</u>. I hadn't met him in a classroom but in a bar; had I, therefore, "gone out of my way to find him"? Not exactly. Through John, one of the other unacceptables, I had encountered a talented, educated, good-looking, jazz pianist. Post-John, I went to Herbie's alone, to hear, I told myself, music. If I tell the truth, though, I was definitely interested in the possibility of seeing Harvey again. And if I did? I knew nothing about him at that point, except he played piano, which was a captivating feature.

An ultimatum, springing from my father's profound exasperation, was issued:

> *Briefly now and to the point. Your recently acquired friendship has been for me the turning point of a very ugly situation. You must now make up your mind whether or not you are a part of this family. You may live with us, if you wish, but if so, you will adhere to a reasonable schedule, sensible activities (precluding any "shocking adventures"), give up your recently acquired so-called friends, and accept life as it is lived in the "sticks" OR, you may leave, move back into another rat-trap and continue with your present interests (whatever the hell they may be). But from the moment of your departure, as far as I am concerned, you are no longer a member of this family. That is to say, I do not wish to hear from you concerning any matter whatsoever, good, bad or indifferent.*
>
> *There is one alternative. If you move to an apartment in an area acceptable to me (and you know damn well what would be acceptable and what wouldn't) and choose friends worthy of*

> *your innate intelligence and basically good background, you will still be our daughter.*

So, years later, I am able to understand that my behavior had caused, legitimately, worry. I'm not referring to the friends I chose, but to my "shocking adventures"; the fact that my father put quotes around this phrase makes me wonder if I had actually characterized my experiences this way, and verbally said so to him. It's more likely, despite the quotation marks, that my father created the term.

His last statement of the take-it-or-leave-it proposition:

> *While you are gritting your teeth and calling me a bastard for the stand I appear to be taking against <u>you</u>, give me a moment to try to show you what you have done to <u>me</u>.*

Then came his "little suicide attempt" paragraph.

My response to the ultimatum was to take my determined self, with its own complex of feelings–disappointment, frustration, anger, dejection–out the door. Having located an apartment in a duplex not that far from Mt. Adams (site of the apartment, which, to validate my father's assessment, had been something of a rat-trap), I was ready to resume adventures, shocking or otherwise.

My new place, a fairly spacious upstairs efficiency in a vividly painted frame house, was furnished, clean, neat. Though I don't remember how I got there with my few belongings, since I was still without a car, I can see myself on the day I settled in, sitting on the sofa re-reading my father's letter, the heart of it so distressing:

> *I am going to try to be perfectly truthful; and therefore, after much, much thought and deliberation I am forced to admit that I am prejudiced, or at very least, a hypocrite. I am not prejudiced according to actual definition, for I have made no biased unreasonable pre-judgment of the negro race. On the contrary, I have always felt that they have gotten the dirty end of the stick. I have argued vehemently for*

their cause (in private discussions)-------but, in all honesty, I must admit that I definitely would take no public stand on the issues involved and I do not wish to become involved myself. So I am a hypocrite. Why am I this way? For the same basic reason that most people are. We react in the same manner to unpleasant situations. We are all egoists, all self-centered. We think firstly of ourselves. I am no crusader, no martyr, no champion of the underprivileged nor any other tritely expressed hero. I am interested only in my own little world (which includes my family, for they are part of me). I am deeply concerned about things which affect me financially, socially and most important of all with things that interfere with my peace of mind.

Interjection: My father did not live long enough to see the marriage of my older, half-Indian daughter to an African American man and the births of my two grandsons, who are half black, a quarter brown, a quarter white...and beautiful, smart, talented.

I had to think about my father and mother, and how true it was that they both were very aloof people, never participating in any kind of community affairs, or joining clubs or church. They were disengaged. But I had barely noticed it until forced to reflect on their various uninvolvements. I thought of my mother's negative and critical stance on just about everything she experienced or witnessed, everything she read in the newspapers or saw on TV. I knew so well my father's extreme cynicism, his propensity to employ sarcasm at every turn. And, since my parents were busy being determinedly removed from society, so was I learning to function in many of the same ways.

The letter I've kept for more than fifty years, periodically re-reading, ended with stabbing words, which, however, bring no memory of tears when I read them in my new apartment in July 1965. Only now, after great time and distance, do I almost cry:

> *How about you becoming unbiased for a moment? Examine the three disapprovals [boyfriends] listed above. Examine the reasons as a disinterested party. THINK!!*
>
> *My days and nights are filled with thoughts of you. Today my work was affected or effected by the constant nagging of questions to myself and no answers. You are affecting my work, my sleep, my <u>life</u>!*
>
> *And---since I am so selfish I've decided not to allow you to cause me such concern. To interfere so with my peace of mind, which took many years to build.*
>
> *I wanted to say so many things. I've said a few. I wanted to be cold and factual. I wanted also to show you how much I really deeply love you and I probably have failed.*
>
> *But I have read it all over --- and basically this is my stand.*
>
> *I expect an answer (an intelligent one).*

Did I give him an answer? I don't know. Did I follow my father's pattern and think firstly of myself? Yes. Though I did not wind up estranged from family, neither did I report or confide anything to them, and my connection with my father was permanently compromised...to be further impaired a few years later at a time when my life had changed dramatically.

Completely infatuated, I deepened my relationship with Harvey, enjoying the jazz, the pot, his warmth, our jouissance. Something was always happening, like the "happening" that Harvey helped organize, which was something new to me. I wasn't sure what it was, but I seem to remember that it took place at the entrance of some kind of culvert where Harvey's musician friends gathered to create the event. Internet info today describes a happening as "a performance, event or situation meant to be considered art, usually as performance art... . Happenings occur anywhere and are often multi-disciplinary, with a nonlinear narrative and the active participation of the audience." I think someone read poetry; Harvey played piano–moving it there had been a feat–his drummer friend Tony set up his drums inside the culvert; someone blew a trumpet...and so it went.

One night Harvey and I and Barry, Harvey's friend who was a philosophy Ph.D. student, sat smoking pot, surrounded by books, in Barry's apartment. As the guys talked, I entered my own daydreaming zone as I let the haze of smoke carry me far from their conversation. Then suddenly–

> How to kéep—is there ány any, is there none such, nowhere known some,
> bow or brooch or braid or brace, láce, latch or catch or key to keep
> Back beauty, keep it, beauty, beauty, beauty, ... from vanishing away?
> Ó is there no frowning of these wrinkles, ranké̀d wrinkles deep,
> Dówn? no waving off of these most mournful messengers, still messengers,
> sad and stealing messengers of grey?
> No there's none, there'ss none, O no there's none...

Barry's voice was strong but a little sad as he was reading the poem, unfamiliar to me, his sound and pace seeming to suit the words and rhythm very well. When he finished, I knew I would never forget the experience of hearing those words.

"What *is* that?" I had been revived by Barry's reading.

"Hopkins," he said, and Harvey smiled.

"Who's Hopkins?" The name was familiar, but I wasn't thinking clearly.

"Gerard Manley Hopkins, nineteenth century British poet. You never heard of him? 'The Leaden Echo and the Golden Echo.'"

I instantly heard *minion,* then *falcon* in my head, words flashing from some dim memory.

"Oh...*morning's minion...*"

"Right. Same guy. That's 'The Windhover.'"

For me, this evening was a happening, spontaneous, unforgettable, a first step on my Hopkins-way to the *terrible* sonnets, a resonating first line–*To seem the stranger lies my lot, my life/Among strangers*–and an image I'd later use for a poem of my own: *poor Jackself.*

A great determination rooted in me as of that night: I would be, because I seemed, the stranger, relishing (when I could) *being,* and being a stranger. I would view the *I* as *she,* she who would be neat and clean, alert and aloof, like the one in a sonnet I once wrote, "Rag Doll":

> The edges of her mind are neatly pinked.
> Worn spots where a mood has played and played
> are patched, the stuffing's plumped, lines are inked
> indelibly. She speaks, as unafraid
> as you or I—*Good morning*—though the day
> is blank and flat. A tightly woven face
> conceals the rags inside. Outside, a gray
> is pressing, naked arms of trees deface
> the cloudless sky, vagrant winds begin
> to yowl. This is the time, the time to yowl.
> She shambles along, steering her head through its din.
> *This is the time, this is the day—now!*
> Then...joining splits with catgut stitches,
> blasé, they mend again, old inner witches.

S-E-X

Pyrite, a mineral, is usually found associated with other sulfides or oxides in quartz veins, sedimentary rock, and metamorphic rock... . Despite being nicknamed fool's gold, it is sometimes found in association with small quantities of gold. (Wikipedia)

Metamorphic rocks arise from the transformation of existing rock types...when subjected to heat and pressure. They make up a large part of the h's crust... .
(Wikipedia)

Animal, Vegetable, or Mineral? was a TV game show my parents watched in the 1950s. For a few years we played the game ourselves, taking turns thinking of an object that the others had to guess, first establishing which of the three categories the thing belonged to. I'd say now, though it wasn't one of my choices in the game then, that sex in the 1950s was, to me, like an object. And if I had to name its category, I'd say it started out in my thinking as mineral: pyrite, something to be found and mined, having taken form from a common human connection that had been subjected to heat and pressure. I spell it now with all caps since everyone thinks it's very important, which, of course, it is. In some senses.

Why pyrite? someone might ask. Why not one of those very precious minerals: rhodium, painite, diamond, black opal, or real gold? It all has to do with placing value;

when I discuss S-E-X here, I distinguish it from gender and biologic assignment. I'm focusing on activity, *having IT*. Yes, I'm viewing activity as an object, one that came to have limited value in my particular ambit of objects.

Initially, S-E-X seemed to have high value, so I looked for it and found it. Because it gleamed, I took it for gold, until I remembered that it came with a host of impurities, the major ones risks of pregnancy, disease, and condemnation. And there was the loss of my own sexual purity, not that I *really* cared about that loss, and couldn't even mark a specific moment I ceased to have an intact hymen. Rough and tumble physical activity had probably stretched it enough so that first-time intercourse produced little pain, no bleeding. But it was hard to dismiss the premium placed on a girl's virginity at that time, and so...after some serious post-coital tristesse set in the night, I kissed my fifteen-year-old purity good-bye. I feared for the life of my reputation, slut-hood being a state I didn't aspire to. After writing about the momentous occasion in a diary I was keeping, I inked out the entry to create a fully blackened page, suspicious of my mother, who had peered, I was certain, into the book previously.

"Going all the way" was the common idiom for the term sexual intercourse at that time, long before "hook-ups" prevailed, and all the way was what I railed against as boyfriend Dick and I indulged in garden variety *petting* (strange term, as if we were *furry* instead of *bare-skinned* animals). Our every movement was hindered by my unpopular words *no* and *stop*. Almost exclusively, our sessions took place in his blue Chevy, parked on some lonely road he had found in his meanderings, and I can still remember the incomparable feeling of mingled desire, excitement, dread, and anger. More than once I leaped out of the car, threatening to walk home, though I had no idea where I was. A couple of times a cop came along, shining his flashlight in the window, illuminating our semi-nude bodies, the height of embarrassment for me. What seemed gold, then, was really fool's gold, something whose value had been diminished by its seeming impurities.

S-E-X, however, was a metamorphic rock, its metamorphosis, as time passed and the pressure increased, resulting in a reclassification. No longer inert, my S-E-X became an animal, very clean and very playful, a cross between a pig (pigs are some of the cleanest animals around) and otter (otters are playful, appearing to engage in various behaviors for sheer enjoyment). And so there was pristine cavorting for a few years.

Not merely metamorphic, S-E-X was metaphoric, standing for an ultimate kind of connection with another human. Eventually, I was fortunate to experience the ULTIMATE-ultimate connection, though it was many, many years after the blue Chevy fumblings.

A bit *precious*, this presentation of S-E-X? *Affectedly concerned with style and metaphor*? But could I do otherwise when the subject at hand is so precious, when lotharios whose stance towards it is, I'd say, affectedly concerned? When it is so valuable, so important men will do anything to get it–including kidnapping and rape? Raping of women, girls, babies, men, crones, sheep, goats, mothers, sisters, cousins, neighbors, dead bodies. And who knows what else?

Precious or not, this is what came to mind when I thought hard about S-E-X.

DESULTORY TIME

"They were *her* years and hers to live as she decided to—as she had to." Reading *Flee the Angry Strangers* by George Mandel, I identified with its female protagonist, Diane Lattimer, and what she felt about her time in the world. At first. But, although she thought she was directing her life, ultimately, she was not. Described on the back of the 1953 book, called the first *beat* novel, as "wild, utterly lost, and only eighteen," Diane slides downhill rapidly, addicted to heroin, whose biting need becomes her director of living.

 I wanted to live my years however I chose, and I think I wanted to be, was being, a little, wild. But I was definitely not lost, and would not become addicted to anything, I was sure. With an incipient consciousness of the need to be resistant to men and their various worlds—professional sports, war, drugs, to name a few of the majors they had created and perpetuated—I knew my way of living had to be entirely mine, nothing simply inherited. I would appropriate only what suited me. A woman could do better than to mimic a man, I was convinced, though many of them did, and do.

 Almost nothing was more horrifying, I thought as I read *Flee the Angry Strangers*, than heroin addiction, its relentless demand, its needles. And junkies were the last men on earth to emulate. At the same time, I castigated addicts, though, I was drinking with abandon, smoking cigarettes, and pot with my boyfriend, jazz pianist Harvey.

"I'd kinda like to be a junkie, just to see what it's like," Harvey said one day after we had been dating about three months.

What? I couldn't believe he was saying that! Suddenly it was over, for me. I didn't care how much I liked him, loved him, or what talents and intelligence he had, how much his smile beguiled me. Didn't care that he was going off to an ivy league school for a Ph.D. The word *junkie* entered my heart like a poisonous arrow, killing with its single thrust my seedling of love for Harvey. Still inept when it came to honest, forthright discourse, I affected a break-up over some paltry wrongdoing on his part, something having to do, I think, with not showing up on time. As in previous endings I had initiated, I behaved in a cowardly fashion, and it would take me many years to gain greater expertise when it came to any confrontations.

Why love one when you can love another? Why pay $90 a month rent when you can pay $35? Changing lovers and living spaces was becoming an exercise in sprezzatura, since I was not, but was attempting to be, like the girl described by literary critic Alfred Kazin in his *Atlantic Monthly* article, "The Girl from the Village": "...she made it a fixed principle to stay loose. She wanted to bring life down to the ultimate in disconnectedness, to make the great refusal of everything that was life to most people, to be always free to move on."

There was nothing nonchalant about my peripeteias. Vaguely aware of how calculated my disconnectedness was, despite any unwillingness to acknowledge it, I must have known the truth about myself: I was not a real drifter. But I threw myself into the part and took a singular pleasure in my accruals: Dick 1–Dave 1–Harvey 1–Dick 2–Jim–Dave 2–John–Harvey 2–Dick 3–Ron–Dave 3, man-wise; and from Upland to Epworth to Oregon to Francis, back to Upland, to Riddle, street-wise. Fidelity and stability were not my states of heart, mind, or dwelling. So I thought.

Ron was longer-lived than some of the others; their tenures were usually about three months. During the early months of this affair, I lived in my second Upland abode, a large house providing a communal kitchen and living room, and shared bedrooms for fifteen young women, many of them students in a stone castle-like building across the street, housing, at the time, an art academy. The shared sleeping arrangements precluded sexual activity, but Ron moved to a nearby city shortly after we started dating, so I'd drive a couple of hours to spend a weekend with him. Since his job came with a company car, he had entrusted me with his own Corvair convertible.

There was never any agreement between Ron and me to date each other exclusively, so when I wasn't visiting him, I was always alert to the possibility of someone new, always someone new. Enter Dave 3. (My time with Dave 2 was so short-lived there are scarcely any details to contribute; I only remember he had a passion for black pepper.)

I met Dave 3 during a trip to the restroom. My insurance company's 15th-floor offices had no facility, and using a restroom necessitated going up or down to the 16th or 14th floor. My habit was to go down, which took me past an open door to the back room of an optician's office where a young guy usually sat making glasses. He was friendly, balding, had a cute smile, and at some point he greeted me, which was the start of yet another 3-month affair, ending with his urging that we not go out with other people. When I didn't respond enthusiastically, he developed his entreaty.

"You know, Seth wants me to go to Bermuda with him. He has a big home there. I don't really want to go, but he keeps on trying to persuade me."

Seth was his rich friend, and Seth was known to be gay. Although I was barely aware of diverse sexual orientations, I intuited that Dave's urging had a subtext: *save me from Seth, save me from myself*. I was not, still am not, a savior-type; our connection was over. I often wonder what path Dave went down.

I had been at the Carew Tower insurance company for about a year when Louis appeared, a young man hired for the same job as mine. I had the assigned task of training him. Two years of college and a year's experience of working for the company to my credit, which Louis didn't have, I was stunned to discover a few months later, as he and I compared notes, that he was being paid five dollars a week more than I was. The sum was not exactly inconsiderable at the time, for me, so I marched my disgruntled self into the vice president's office. *Why*, I wanted to know, was I being paid less than this upstart (I didn't actually use that word). The VP seemed a bit startled that I knew it and was, moreover, so bold as to confront him with it. This was before feminism's consciousness-raising had affected the general population regarding equal pay (whose equal-ness still eludes women).

I remember the VP's avuncular response, the benevolence of which was all for my colleague, none for me:

> "Louis is a family man now he's married. You may not know it, but he has two kids to support; his new wife already had these little ones when they married. So, you see, he needs that extra pay."

Although I reined in my wrath, refraining from saying what I really felt, that Louis' situation didn't affect me, I did say a few words about my own needs, and, especially, my definition and strong expectations of fairness. But speaking out was futile, and I left the VP's office, going on to bide my time for a couple of months so as to take a two-week vacation that I had earned. Then I quit the job.

Fort Lauderdale, Florida. A vacation without parents, my first—what freedom! It was 1966, the year when I finally understood that when it came to romance, I was interested, almost exclusively, in beginnings, which afforded me the most pleasure. One, the *sui generis,* took place during this Florida sojourn. I had spread a towel on the beach across from The Roost, a motel where I was staying, and, always on the lookout for good-looking men, I did my usual quick scan of the immediate environs. Perspicacious, I knew to mostly favor intelligence over hunkiness; the very good-looking, my conviction, were often excessively arrogant.

I was lying on my towel, eyes closed against the sun since no one was around to pique my interest. Vigilant against sunburn, I sat up after a while to change my position and happened to look to my right, where rather far down the beach stood a young, tan, dark-haired man. The distance was great enough to rule out eye-contact, but, since he was facing my direction, I imagined he was looking at me. It was not implausible, I considered, my body being in good shape, quite tanned after weeks of gradual sunning in Ohio in preparation for Florida's greater beams. And men do like bodies!

It's easy to stare when you don't know for sure if someone's staring back. And so I did. For a minute. Then I stretched out on the towel again on my side, facing this guy whose features were still indistinct. If there is to be a seduction, I mused, who would seduce whom?

I shut my eyes...but not for long. When I opened them, it seemed as though he had edged closer, and though my posture suggested, I'm sure, relaxation, the excitement I had been feeling through the first week of an unchaperoned holiday bubbled even stronger. I still couldn't see his face clearly but his body was on the order of *stunning*. After what seemed a protracted, tantalizing, inch-by-inch approach, he stood by me.

"Hi." Could there be a more thrilling word, I wondered?

"Hello." Nothing else came to mind in my state of near paralysis. Resplendent, this guy!

He sat right down in the sand beside my towel, which was too small to share. Funny how I have no memory of his next words; I would have thought they'd be etched in my mind, like his face is. He was what someone today might call, I suppose, a *hot dude*. As it developed, though, Dick 3 (another Dick!) was definitely not pepper-hot. (Number two had been one of those exceedingly handsome specimens with its coincident arrogance. He was, therefore, short-loved and not worth particularizing.) This Dick was rather sweet, a bit shy, and seemingly a non-macho type of gentle, all qualities bringing into question my good-looks theory.

Despite those first words having flown off somewhere, I remember everything else that happened: dinner together that night; sleeping with him (he was staying in The Roost too); breakfast with him the next morning; then every breakfast, lunch, dinner and night together for the six remaining days of his vacation. He had come from New York with his friend Ben and had only one week in the sun. I spent those days hanging out with him and, sometimes, Ben, whose words I do remember. Looking at me, he said to Dick,

"She's the kind of girl you take home to your parents."

I remember being uncertain as to whether I was pleased or annoyed. A little of both, I'm sure.

Walking on the beach at night, palm fronds splayed against the sky, Dick's hand holding mine as my sun-bleached hair blew around, I savored the salt air, the moment, my youth. For the time being, I had the appreciation of one of the world's more handsome men, one whose other qualities just might be, I speculated, sterling, too. Lucky, I'm lucky. Yes, if it has to *be*, life should be just this good.

After my vacation I had to find another job. *A secretary?* At one time it was inconceivable, but when I, an employment-seeker, sat completing an agency's application and was told that the employee-seeker at the next desk needed one and wanted to speak to me, I sat down next to him. Discovering that his offer was immediate and came at $90 a week (when I had been making $75), I capitulated and promptly quit my underwriter-trainee job at the insurance company.

Was I really going to be someone's secretary? I thought on my first day on the new job. I self-counseled: get over it, take the money each week, zone out whenever you can; one stupid job will not be a significant milestone on the journey to mature identity. My antidote for feeling poisoned was carrying a newly-purchased book of modern poetry to work each day for lunch-time reading.

Working for Charlie Stamp turned out to be extraordinarily uncomplicated, the office consisting of boss/owner Charlie, a salesman, a repair man, and me, the one woman. My daily chores included answering the phone that rang infrequently, typing up very few orders and invoices, and refusing to serve the men coffee. They did not include going out cocktail-lounging with the salesman, which is what I did. Foolishly.

Two days after the lounging, I woke up bored and discontented, loath to go be a secretary for one more day, after three months of forbearance. I decided I was going to drive to New York. Getting to Greenwich Village had been my objective for two years, so why not use my beachboy as a way to get established there? Dick and I were still connected, and I had flown to New York twice to visit him.

I began loading my car-on-loan (Ron's Corvair), and just when I thought I had completed the task, making sure the seven dollars to my name was in my purse with my credit card, I was interrupted.

"Oh, my god, you're alive!" she threw her arms around me, my downstairs neighbor Jill from the swinging-singles apartment complex I now lived in on Riddle Road.

Perplexed, I agreed with her.

"Your mother called your office, and they said you hadn't come in yet, so she called me. She was so worried that the strangler had gotten you."

Seems there was a Cincinnati strangler attacking women in our university neighborhood.

"No," I confirmed, "not yet."

Having proved I was intact, I decided I should pay a quick visit to my mom before setting out, so I drove my borrowed, packed-up car to her house.

What in our rare mother-daughter conversation persuaded me to abandon my impulsive travel plan, I've always wondered. Maybe nothing. Maybe the specter of a strangler set me off-balance. I don't know, but I scrapped the New York scheme, drove home, caught a late morning bus to work, and got to the office after my three male associates, all morning lollygaggers usually, had already started working.

The boss was in his office. Soon he buzzed and I found myself standing before him, reluctantly.

"There's a way you can keep your job," he informed me, after laying out my transgression: not arriving to work that day on time.

I could keep my job if I *went out with him* (translate, *have sex* with him). Quitting a job without another in hand is not prudent, but it was all I could do with the outrage I felt as I slammed out of the office and deserted Charlie.

Postscript, 2015. Out of curiosity I googled Charlie Stamp and found some interesting info. Apparently, he devolved into an abusive husband and his wife hired someone to kill him. The plan didn't work, though, and the wife was caught and convicted of attempted murder.

Jobless, but pleased to be non-secretarial, I was free to join the weekly happy hour hosted by one of the swinging-single guys in my apartment building, who ended his work-week each Friday at noon. Oh, those salesmen! A quite different species from the secretary. I showed up on time and began plying myself with one of my then-favorite drinks: Echo-and-soda. Echo Spring bourbon with club soda, that is. I think I mainly liked not the taste but saying *Echo-and-soda*.

A likely consequence of living by one tenet of my creed, *expect nothing,* was the assured *unexpected*, which could be very satisfying, if not glorious, like sunbeams piercing through dull cloud cover on a day threatening to be dreary from dawn to dusk. Such was the denouement of my first unemployed Friday after losing that disagreeable secretary status.

It was the first time I had seen someone drop a lobster into a pot of boiling water, watched its dirt-brown turn fire-red. That's one impressive thing I remember seeing on October 21, 1966. Another, and far more significant, was the lobster-dropper himself, a young man like no other I had ever met: PhD student, handsome, Asian Indian.

Happy hour in the salesman's apartment had been terminated when my roommates urged me to freshen up, change clothes, and accompany them to a University of Cincinnati campus party. I was apathetic, but willing. Uninhibited when I got to the party, still affected by my glut of Echo-and-sodas, I took one look around, spotted the lobster man and began following him throughout the small apartment, eventually cornering him, literally: his chair in a corner was barricaded by mine in front of him.

"Do you ever think about acorns?"

He didn't answer my left-field question—such an absurd conversation-starter—but I can still see his smile, outstanding. Despite the cockamaminess of my approach, surprising even to me, it worked. By the end of the evening this guy who said his name was Shah had asked me to go to a movie the following weekend. But before that weekend arrived, he called on Wednesday, inviting me to go with him for ice cream.

"What's your last name?" I asked as we sat at Howard Johnson's over coconut ice cream.

"Shah."

"Your name's Shah Shah?!" I knew nothing about Indian names.

Then he told me that his first name was difficult for Americans to pronounce correctly so he went by his surname.

"What *is* your first name?"

"Gautam."

An ancient name, in Sanskrit it meant *one who dispels darkness* (ignorance) *by his brilliance* (spiritual knowledge). Before Buddha became enlightened, I learned, he was known as *Siddhartha*; afterwards, *Gautama*. Turned out that this Gautam I had met had a younger brother named Siddharth. Always enthralled by names, I was in love with these, new to me, but like his American friends I took the easy way out and called him Shah. As he explained, the "t" sound in Gautam was not the same as in English, being close to "th," but not quite that either.

Lobster–acorn–ice-cream–movie: by this means my new life was set in motion, and progressed at breakneck speed: meeting, October 21; first date, October 26; proposal,

December 8. I had dodged steadiness, then marriage, for a few years; Gautam had determined he would not get involved with an American woman. Then, in the midst of great unexpectations...

In college, much to the dismay of my tradition-bound, engaged-to-be-married roommate Jane, I divulged my true character at a dorm dinner one night when one of the girls announced she had gotten *pinned* to her boyfriend, saying something to the effect that I would never get pinned, engaged, or married.

"I'd rather be someone's mistress than wife," I declared, "since she has all the fun and romance, none of the drudgery, enslavement."

"Even if you believe in it, *free love*," Jane rebuked me later, "do you have to tell people?"

I wish I had been able to say what I was thinking, that anyone truly free to love would not waste the emotion on someone like Bucky, her less than charming fiancé. But my outspokenness had its limits; I could readily speak for myself but didn't like to criticize someone else's choices.

Bucky was obnoxious, though, and worse: possessive, dictatorial, cold and commanding. A mean gleam in his eye, controlling Jane's every move, he had all the makings of an abusive husband. She had to have breakfast, lunch, and dinner with him, devote all her non-study time to him, then study with him as well. If I had known then what I know now about such guys, I would have placed money on his devolving into a batterer, at the very least.

Two becoming one? Living as a number 9B pencil drawing, my outline shadowed, blurred, smudged into a husband? Was that the purpose of love—*blurring*? Convinced I was too rock-solid hard for the likes of obfuscation, I clung to my notion of free loving as the best loving.

I was not going to get married. I was going to get, somehow, to Greenwich Village, where I assumed all the artists and poets lived, where I would find my milieu. Not for me the life of wife. Not for me the responsibilities of home and hearth, kids and cooking. No.

"Will you marry me?" Gautam asked as we sat with drinks in a bar called King's Row.

What?! I was shocked. Then...
"Yes," no hesitation.

We married. Eloped, since I would have nothing to do with the institution of wedding, the wearing of a white dress, the symbolic passing of a woman from father to husband: no. In fact, refusing to buy anything special for the occasion, I wore an orange wool dress, orange suede shoes, both having been worn to work frequently. I informed no one ahead of time about the ceremony, which was performed without witnesses by a justice of the peace.

Two weeks into marriage my father called me, just to check in and see how I was.

"What's new?"

"Oh, nothing much," I responded, "but I did get married recently." Of course, I knew how startling it sounded.

"It's your daughter," my father said (my mother must have been nearby), "she's married. Do you want to talk to her?"

She declined, refusing for a month thereafter to talk with me, in spite of the fact I had always said that if for some reason I went against my decree and *did* marry, no one would hear from me. I had made no secret of the fact that I spurned nuptials, veils, and vows.

My mother and I never had a conversation about marriages and weddings when I was young, and we didn't have one post-marriage, so I don't know if she was a mother who had ever had an expectation of my walking down the aisle gowned and veiled. I don't think so, but neither do I know why she was reticent for so long after I eloped. Was she, on some level, disappointed? Did she feel shut out? Pissed off? Was she averse to my marrying an Indian man? I never found out, never asked her. Our relationship was not conducive to any heart-to-heart talks, nor brain-to-brain. And we were not the kind of family that processed things in retrospect; things happened; we all moved on. Clearly, though, my contempt for the institution of marriage had been discounted, and rightly so. I was married.

Single life, apartment with roommates, liberty—all were left behind as I began cohabiting with my first man ever, about whose worthiness there was no question. He was sterling, a well-made male: responsible, productive, kind, loving; there could be, I was sure, no better husband. If only I had truly wanted a husband.

I liked the layout of our little home, a one-bedroom apartment, charming, cozy, with an arched doorway from living room to dining nook and kitchen, bedroom at the back. The constant nearness of another being in a small space, though, was unfamiliar, and not altogether pleasing. It was strange, I felt, to be living with someone male, someone with whom I was to be regularly intimate. Nonetheless, I was so happy to have a piano for the first time since leaving my parents' home, having immediately rented one after moving in, and I lost no time finding a teacher to study with, having had only three years of lessons as a child.

Playing it incessantly, Chopin's "Prelude #20" with its deep melancholy tones, soothing to me (unaware that it was known as the *funeral march*), I could almost forget there were household chores that, like meddling neighbors, insinuated themselves into my days. Cooking, which was appealing; cleaning, which was not. And laundry, that three-headed monster always clawing at me with its wash-iron-fold imperative. Notwithstanding domestic tedium, though, I tried for marital bliss, which was not to be had, my fault entirely.

One night, reluctant to go to bed, I preferred staying with Chopin at the piano, then *Dr. Zhivago* on the sofa, and my passivity prompted a quarrel, whose particulars I've long forgotten but whose outcome is forever stamped in my memory.

Exasperated, Gautam slapped me.

We went to bed, morning came, I left our apartment. And never returned. Having grown up in fear of a woman, my mother, I would not live in fear of a man, which held the risk of even worse ill-treatment. More fortunate than many women who might feel compelled to leave a man but have nowhere to go, no resources to draw upon, I was able to move back with my parents, however undesirable that measure seemed. No, I concluded I didn't want to be married. So what if I was to have a baby?

I'm lying in bed waiting, listening, for my father to come home, pull his car into the driveway. Home is a lower room of the new split-level house my parents bought when I moved back with them, where I've lived now without my husband for three months, waiting for our baby to be born. I wait, in a state of suspension, married, pregnant, separated, dating my husband–we go to lunch, dinner, movies–a confluence of circumstances perplexing to my mother. I understand her confusion.

After I left him, Gautam persuaded my father that I must need psychiatric treatment, or some such thing. Although skeptical, insisting that my behavior was normal for me, my father went along with the idea of my seeing a professional, which I did. After some discussion, the guy wrote on my new chart "no therapy indicated." I suspected that, anticipating support for the notion that I was *deranged*, both my husband and father were frustrated; I wasn't sorry to disappoint them. In retrospect, I could have suggested that the slapping incident, arising from a desire to "show superiority over me," as Gautam later confessed in a letter to me, was evidence of dysfunctional comportment. Of course, it was simply a classic business-as-usual kind of technique, so often employed by men.

It's late. I wait, knowing my father will not be sober when he gets in, whenever that is; it's golf night. My mother's former tactic of driving him to the golf course and picking him up after the game is obsolete, the household a two-car family now. Powerless to change the inevitable sequence of door slam, stagger, and clamor, all I can think is *how did I get myself in this position of unwilling witness again?* In the eighth month of pregnancy, I have some difficulty sleeping anyway, and now...my old childhood curse of sleeplessness in the face of impending tumult is on me. So I'm caught in a web of ruminations: what will happen when the baby's here, will I try marriage again, what will motherhood be like, where will I live, will I ever be able to go back to college...?

I hear a car. I tense and listen. Yes, he's home. I can't stand this another time, so I leave my bed and go into the bathroom where there is a small crawl space, taking a blanket and pillow with me. I close the bathroom door, squeeze into the space, close its door. Maybe I won't have to hear the wrangling this time.

When I go into labor at 2 a.m. on November 6, my parents drive me to the hospital, and Gautam meets me there. I'm excited but casual about the whole birth process, convinced that in general, women have made too much of it and that I'll pop the baby out and be on my way. Not having experienced menstrual cramps, ever, and therefore discounting what I consider *palaver* about them, I'm positive that childbirth trauma has been overplayed as well.

Six hours pass, and I'm moved from my private room to the labor room, still cool, calm, having little information, no understanding about *labor*.

"George! Help me! Let me go home...no!...no!...I can't do this! Mama! Help me! George! George!" This hysterical woman next to me is clearly in distress, and I begin to worry, just a little. Still certain that I'm too strong, too tolerant, too tough to be brought to such a ridiculous state of elaborated suffering, I register, nonetheless, the fact that my own contractions have grown a bit more pronounced.

Another six hours go by, and I'm appalled that resident doctors, all male, keep coming into the room to do an internal exam just when a contraction is at its peak.

"No, not now!" I yell. But that is just, I'm informed, when they have to check my progress.

The help-me-George woman is gone, and I'm the only one in the room, the only one screaming. And I go right on screaming for a final three hours, until at some point a couple of nurses bring Gautam into the room, which makes me scream louder than ever.

"Get him out of here!" Unlike George-woman, I don't want a husband around during my personal hell-time.

It's a very good thing that arrogant people are subject to comeuppances. I certainly got mine, and with it a measure of empathy that has lasted throughout my life as I understand now the magnitude of childbirth pain at times, like my time, whose total labor was about twenty-one hours, six of those being very hard, the last three unbearable, though I had to endure, all birthing women have to endure, even the unbearable.

And then...new baby next to me on the gurney, I'm being wheeled out of delivery and back to my own room, the doctor walking along beside me, chatting as though we're leaving a party. It's a wonder he doesn't ask if I've had a good time. What he does ask is whether I've ever had any pain medication before. *No*, I say.

"Well, you had enough to put anyone else completely under," he smiles. "I thought I might have to do a caesarean, but you pulled through." He looks down at the baby. "She's a cutie!"

Sometimes it's hard to tell just how cute a newborn is, so looking at her somewhat red, wrinkled condition, I'm dubious, but the next day, as I study her face, I conclude that the pronouncement is more than accurate: she's definitely cute. There is little doubt about my baby's beauty, however much someone may want to insist that a prejudiced-mother attitude has taken over. In spite of her father's desire to name her *Zarina,* I insist on *Tanya* (with Zarina as a middle name), same as Dr. Zhivago's wife, since I had been reading the novel during pregnancy and like the name. I don't realize, at first, that my new Tanya was born on the eve of the Russian revolution. As it turns out, my mother thinks the name is a strange choice, claims she can't remember it, and calls her Sonia for awhile.

The month just before Tanya's birth I was reading a book that seems to have been dismissed and forgotten now: *Finnley Wren* by Philip Wylie, a writer I had heard mentioned by an aunt of mine when she referred to his 1942 book, *Generation of Vipers*, a vitriolic condemnation of American culture. From *Finnley Wren*, I wrote in my quote book what I viewed as wise words:

> *You can't possess a person—any more than you can actually possess property. It's there. You can enjoy it. But pick it up, carry it around, put it in your pocket—no. When you leave property is there for others. When you die it's still there. You can own nothing on this earth, least of all another human being.*

This baby that's mine is not *mine*. I hope that as I do my mothering I'll remember that, and I remind myself of my tenet: *expect nothing*. I feel sure that parents who have great expectations for their kids are risking a letdown.

INDIA, 1968

I. Wonderful, Awful

Ph.D. in hand, job with Exxon lined up, my husband returned to India for his first visit in six years before his U.S. work life in New Jersey was to begin. After learning about me, his family arranged for me to travel to India, so we could all meet. I flew with my three-month-old baby to Bombay, as the city was called before its name officially changed to *Mumbai* in 1995.

For me, India was wonderful and awful, fascinating and deplorable. Everything was alien, but fascinating: crowds, sounds, sights, smells, tastes, language, customs, traffic, clothes, hairstyles... .

"I'm a grown woman; I can pack my own bags!" My husband and his older brother bend over my suitcase, intent on packing it for our trip to Ahmedabad, where we would attend a cousin's wedding. I protest what I consider interference, stand my ground, which sparks amusement and perplexity on their part. But I don't care; I know I have to set limits from the start and do. As time passes, I'll learn to discern when to capitulate or compromise, when to insist on defending what I deem my rights.

Our stay in Ahmedabad has us visiting various relatives, one of whom is an aunt known to have been at odds through the years with my mother-in-law. We are invited, however, to her home for tea, probably because she wants to look me over; as an American woman, I incite much curiosity. After the preliminary greeting and introduction, we settle in her living room and tea is served.

"You trapped him, didn't you?" is this aunt's first utterance, looking directly at me as though conducting an interview to determine my worthiness, or lack thereof, for admission to the extended family. Not fully fluent in English, she has enough words at her command to formulate the allegation.

I don't flinch. "Yes, I did."

There are a few smiles through the room, then the conversation takes another turn. She is not completely ungracious, though, presenting me, when we depart, with a gift I still have: a hand-embroidered cloth that now hangs from one of my bookcases.

Curiosity about me is most often apparent in the children. At the wedding we attend, a boy, maybe seven or eight years old, follows me throughout the reception, sitting at my feet when I sit, gazing up at me. Doubtlessly, he has never seen anyone who looks quite like me. Another time, as I'm walking down a road, school girls pass by in a line, staring and staring. The last girl turns her head to continue scrutinizing me, trips and almost falls.

Perhaps the most poignant moment I experience is when the long-time family servant, Madhu, declines my mother-in-law's suggestion that he carry my baby out to the streets for a little walk, shaking his head. *Why*, we want to know. In his language, Marathi, he explains, earnestly, that she is too beautiful, and he's afraid someone might cast an evil eye on her. This is the same man who launders her diapers and irons them each afternoon, a humble, kind, hard-working man, who is sometimes unfairly subject to my mother-in-law's harsh beratings.

"Mummy wants you to come into the kitchen and do puja," my younger brother-in-law tells me one day. "It's Lord Krishna's birthday."

No, I'm not going to pray to Krishna any more than I would pray to Christianity's god.

"You know I'm an atheist. I can't do that," I smile, and he smiles back, leaving the living room to carry the message to his mother. I think she already understands it's a lost cause trying to get me to embrace a Hindu god. There are no repercussions.

Curious to see if there were any reports from other Americans who had traveled to India, I hung out in a New Jersey library one day after returning to the states and came upon *An American in India* (1954), by J. Saunders Redding, professor at Brown University and first African American faculty member to teach at an Ivy League university. Detailing his experiences during a U.S. State Department assignment to India, he wrote:

> It takes a long time for a Westerner in India to learn a very important thing: all the adjustments he has to make are primary, and only seldom can he stop making them. His nerves wind tight, lose resilience, and lie exposed to shock like a coil of worms caught in the pitiless glare of the sun. Everything that touches them puts them in danger of crumbling, and everything touches them–the poverty, which is a gross exaggeration of all he knows as poverty; the outrageous multiform swarm of life rooted in a million customs, anomalous manners, taboos, laws; the people. Especially the people who, with all their consciousness of kind, seem to think of themselves less as a people than a force. They create an atmosphere of driving tension similar to that one feels in the power housing of a mighty ship steaming full speed ahead. If the Western foreigner is not careful, he will carry this tension around with him. One has to try to relax from it at every opportunity and as quickly as one can.

The tension he described was exactly what I had felt; I, too, quickly understood the necessity for relaxing from it. As one who had *married* an Indian, I had the further challenge of habituating myself to a family culture where individualism, especially for a woman, was subsumed by the machinery of the family.

II. Covers, Camouflage, Curtains

White Gandhi cap on his head, paan further staining his already red mouth, the tailor sat cross-legged on the sun porch floor running a Singer sewing machine, its whirring accented by an occasional caw from a crow perched on the open window frame. Mummy had hired him to sew blouses and petticoats for all the many new saris she had bought me. I had arrived in India sari-less, of course; moreover, I had very little clothing at all, due to my suitcase being filled with a supply of baby formula.

Fascinated by this foreign luxury of a tailor making house calls, I was soon exasperated by the difficulty of adapting to sari-style dressing. Obligingly though, round my body I wrapped, pleated, and tucked one end of six yards of fabric into a petticoat, draping over my shoulder the other end, about twenty inches or so of cloth, called a *palav*, often elaborately embroidered. Every day for six weeks I braved the struggle to keep it all in place as I sat down, stood up, moved around, and squatted over an Indian hole-in-the-floor arrangement at places having no western-style toilet.

Ignorant of the various modes of wearing a sari, I expressed, when asked for it, my preference: the Bengali style worn by my sister-in-law, not the Gujerati style of my mother-in-law and her sisters. Mummy scowled but didn't make an issue of it. I suspected, though, that any way *I* wore a sari would underscore a lack of natural feminine grace, and I always felt awkward, inept, and unworthy in the gorgeous cottons and silks.

During a second trip to India in 1970, I was brazen enough to wear bell-bottomed jeans and miniskirts, foregoing the sari imperative except for dinners and weddings. I bought a few *lungis* (tubular waist-to-floor sarongs) and *kufnis* (long shirts), which I relished wearing back home where I rarely saw Indian women, at that time in the early seventies–and certainly no Americans–covering themselves in such unconventional garments. In fact, the lungi, while worn by both men and women in India, seemed most common among males who were physical laborers, though I was unbothered by that. From having been a young girl briefly enamored of fashion, I had become one who would not follow prescriptive fashion or tradition, having recognized the cultural manipulation, in both the east and west, that kept women fixated on how to cover themselves, which color and style reigned in a particular season, and what was *appropriate*. So even though I had loved clothes as much as the next girl-teen, by my twenty-somethings I would not be duped. Idiosyncratically, I covered my nakedness, always attracted to the slightly offbeat, a favorite garment in the 1970s being a cornflower blue and cream striped mini-skirted knit dress with a detachable, floor-length overskirt, much like a cape, that tied at the waist.

Conspicuous among the five thousand or so mammal species for being naked (having lost our fur a million years ago), not to mention ashamed and law-breaking when minus our covers in public, we humans have been wearing clothing for 170,000 years. What followed the manufacture of covering materials, ranging from cotton, linen, silk, wool, to synthetics, was a fashion industry comprised of designers, tailors, and *toothpicks*, aka *women*, festooned and sashaying down runways with sundry *looks*, boredom a key aspect since looking like they'd seen and done everything was thought to be very cool. One extreme of this coolness, the peculiar *heroin chic* aesthetic of the 1990s, employed ads featuring pale, ultra-thin models whose dark-circled eyes and messy, knotted hair was supposed to make them look like addicts. But even before this aesthetic, there was the mid-19th century ideal, a pale face, which propelled some white women to rub their faces with breadcrumbs; eat chalk, slate and tea grounds; suck on lead pencils; or sip vinegar. These were all tactics said to achieve an extreme-pale epitome of white-skin beauty.

Fashion ads for heroin chic included images of highly sexualized, bruised, bloodied, and even dead women–displays whose shocking details are meant to capture attention, which actually divert me from the clothing. All I can see is one more bit of evidence for just how much women, both models and potential consumers, have been manipulated, and have allowed the manipulation, in a reigning vogue governed by the hubris and greed of men. With great satisfaction, then, I look back on my early decision to reject fashion and the possible profession of designer, disgust being my overwhelming feeling in the face of perversion and exploitation.

I have never shown cleavage. A choice. Maybe the wearing of bathing suits had me with a bit of it, but otherwise, no. Not even when I wore a strapless evening gown to a prom when I was fourteen, that netted dress, though strapless, having a generous, substantial, snug bodice. But what an uncomfortable night it was, me worried and tugging at the top, fearful of having even one iota of exposure, which might engender one bit of ridicule––I knew that boys could be cruelly disparaging of a female body. The dress, not of my choosing, was a hand-me-down from my cousin, and I was grateful to have it, but a few years later, when I was a prom queen candidate, my grandparents took me shopping for a dress of my own. With a straight-across-the-chest bodice, the dress I chose had the assured support of spaghetti straps, which kept me at ease throughout the prom.

 I love my breasts, especially the fact that they were the means by which I could feed my second baby, Zarina. Poor Tanya suffered allergies since I elected not to nurse her, listening to misguided advice.

 "You don't want to do that," my mother had said. "You feel like a cow. And, besides, it's old-fashioned."

 I bought it, although now I think *how could doing what the female human is built to do ever be old-fashioned?* With Tanya, I had to try four different formulas before coming upon one that didn't cause skin rash or diarrhea.

 Feeding Zarina, I did not feel like a cow, not knowing, anyway, what a cow feels like. Especially when it's being milked, like it or not, by human hands or machines.

 One paramount truth about breasts is that they've been fetishized...or ridiculed: for being too small–to the point of fostering a desire for implants; too large—to the point of seeking surgical reduction; too old and droopy; too female-ish. And when disease mandates removal, they are commonly reconstructed. Let no woman be without them! Perversely, breasts have also been a focal point of men's lust, and yet, considered obscene if used anywhere in public for their true purpose. A multitude of slang words have been devised for breasts, none of them sounding complimentary: tits, titties, boobs, hooters, jugs, knockers, et al. There is, too, an off-putting lexicon for bra: flopper-stopper; double-barreled slingshot; hooter harness; over-the-shoulder-boulder-holder. Me show any part of my breasts, or the hollow between them, in the face of Toms, Dicks, and Harrys? No! And it's very agreeable to be old and uncompromising now, though, I was equally obdurate when young.

As I grow old and the ascendant *look* of a woman becomes more and more sexualized—tight, short skirts; low necklines; stilettos; long, long hair—my defiance intensifies.

"It's so hot today," I might complain.

"Well, why don't you take off that shirt?!" Someone could respond. That is, the shirt over my shirt, which camouflages my body, the overshirt I learned to wear when I was young. This is cloth that feels protective, a barrier to any lascivious or scornful gazes from any nefarious spectators or miscreants in our current *rape culture* (environment in which rape is prevalent, perpetuated through the use of misogynistic language, objectification of women's bodies, and glamorization of sexual violence—thereby creating a society that disregards women's rights and safety).

All new saris were packed when I was ready to leave India after that first visit, though I thought it unlikely I'd wear many again, most of the pastel colors and unremarkable designs, in contrast to the gorgeous, more typically Indian colors and patterns, not to my liking. But in awe of my mother-in-law's generosity, I didn't want to reject them, which would have meant risking her disapproval anyway, so back in New Jersey, I set up my sewing machine and soon our naked apartment windows had curtains.

INVASIONS, 1970

April 30. U.S. troops invade Cambodia. Hundreds of university, college, and high school campuses shut down because of student strikes, violent and non-violent protests, more than 4 million students involved.

I'm at Rutgers University, Newark, New Jersey, having started during the fall of 1969 to finish my undergraduate degree; my final exams are cancelled after the invasion.

May 4. National Guardsmen invade a crowd of student protesters at Kent State University, firing at them and killing four, wounding nine.

June. My mother files for divorce. She's tired of my father's drinking; he is tired of her. As my father says in a letter he sends my husband, "had there been no children, it is doubtful that the marriage would have lasted more than two or three years." But, for twenty-seven, they suffered together, "poor, incompatible, never-should-have-married-in-the-first-place" people, as my father described them, with insurmountable problems. "I am a certain type of individual; she is the antithesis of this type, and always will be. And I damn well am not going to change!"

I fly to India for my second visit, planning to study at the University of Bombay for a semester, taking Tanya, who is not yet three years old, with me. I arrive in time to attend my brother-in-law's wedding; the aftermath further raises my consciousness about cultural differences, especially in the *joint family* arrangement where two or more generations of people reside together.

When my new sister-in-law enters the household, she can do nothing right, consistently being relegated to that damned-if-you-do, damned-if-you-don't realm for her perceived shortcomings; you might say her arrival is an invasion of our mother-in-law's territory. If she sleeps too late and isn't in the kitchen to help prepare the elaborate lunch that is always served, she's *lazy*. If she gets up very early and is in there peeling and chopping the vegetables, she's *making Mummy look bad.* Prone to the adult version of tantrums, Mummy sometimes retreats to her bedroom, closing the door, refusing to come out.

Such is, I learn, the common mother-in-law/daughter-in-law tribulation in Indian families, where the former, who has once been the latter and suffered, waits to be the one in power; traditionally, it is the extent of a woman's power. But both my sisters-in-law are highly educated, the older one having a medical degree, the younger a law degree, a fact that was probably vexatious to Mummy, who married at age fourteen.

I'm also subject to tyranny, but as an American still largely ignorant of the ins and outs of Indian customs, I can bask in my ignorance, which saves me, I believe, from the full force of any possible wrath. Knowing, though, that my sister-in-law and brother-in-law are leaving soon for the U.S. and that I could be the next butt of any grievances Mummy might have, I plan my escape, having as a credible excuse to cut short my visit, my own sister's wedding, taking place in September. So I fly home, regretting the early termination of my studies.

May to September. Brother marries, parents divorce, sister marries. After my return from India, Gautam, Tanya, my brother-in-law, sister-in-law and I drive from New Jersey to Cincinnati to attend my sister's wedding, invading my parents' house, which has not sold yet though the divorce is final. Interesting environment––parents still residing together, father dating, new arrivals from India who are fascinated by TV.

"Are they still watching?" my father says to me after coming home from a date.

I'm defensive. "Don't forget, it's new for them."

Somehow, we all get through the various ordeals of being together for a few days, celebrating a wedding in the face of a dissolution. The newspaper carries, on the same day, both the announcement of my sister's marriage and my parents' divorce.

Thanksgiving. My father is a fan of Lauren Bacall, the star in a musical, *Applause,* which is playing on Broadway. Inviting him to New Jersey for Thanksgiving, I promise to buy tickets. He drives from Cincinnati, stopping for dinner somewhere along the way, probably drinking more than he should have, arriving later than expected. The next morning, Saturday, he decides to go to Aqueduct Racetrack in Queens and takes off early, coming home just in time for us to go to dinner and the play. While his behavior doesn't suggest he's inebriated, neither can I judge his level of sobriety.

Gautam arrives with the babysitter for Tanya, and we head to the city. I remember nothing about the ride, nothing about dinner, nothing about the play. But what I can't forget is what happens after we return home, while Gautam's taking the babysitter home. My father and I are sitting on the sofa talking. For some reason I recall one irrelevant detail: the dress I was wearing, which I had sewn from a shiny fabric, its design and sundry colors rather psychedelic–fitting for the 1970s–a blue somewhere between dark and bright being the dominant color. I suppose we're talking about New York, the restaurant, the play, I don't know.

It's a most sudden thing, most intrusive, so startling that I can't relive the previous moment or much of the subsequent conversation, abbreviated since I run out the door, heading for the parking lot to wait for my husband. I only remember the thrust of my father's tongue invading my mouth.

It might as well be an albatross hung around my neck: the white dove dominating the pale gray paperback cover of *Modern European Poetry*, permanent reminder of my father's transgression. Peace offering, atonement—is that what he intends it to be, this gift my father buys me before leaving New Jersey? I am not pacified. I didn't, and don't, forget. Nor do I ever use the word *forgive,* so tinged with religiosity, so apt to imply that everything's okay. Everything was, is, not okay, nor is there a word to convey my subsequent feeling for, and behavior toward, a father I once adored, then admired, even after disillusionment, finally reviled, though failed to hate. There is neither war nor peace between us, only nervous neutrality. I continue to feel something, something resembling love but far removed. More nearly estranged than ever, we maintain a distant relationship, but never again do I feel the kind of love for him that I felt as a child, keeping him at more than arm's length, emotionally and in actuality.

That morning-after when my father leaves, I sit down and begin to thumb through the book he has given me, quickly coming upon, by chance, a short poem titled "You Disappear" by Jules Supervielle:

> Already closed in mist you disappear...
> There are dead leaves all along your way
> Stirred by the failing breath of loves gone by...

I put the book away. For years, I never look at it.

The letter I write my father about his violation is, like his to me in 1965, "not a work of art" and has "very little literary value." Nor is its main issue "cleverly disguised." I address, head-on, his conduct toward me, naming the offense, quoting the one thing I remember his saying at the time: "Don't you believe in incest?" I describe other incidents I learned of, letting him know that I'm aware of what took place after a party he threw in the wake of my mother's divorcing him and moving out of their house. Behavior beyond my comprehension or willingness to put into words.

I threaten to have him "forcibly removed to a hospital" if he doesn't see a psychiatrist, assuring him that I mean it. My letter sounds pompous:

> When I return from my vacation on January 7, I expect to have received some communication from you telling me your doctor's name, address, telephone number and the progress you have made in your sessions with him.... I will be standing by ready to receive any letters from you if you feel the need to write about anything.

We have a phone conversation in which my father says he guesses he needs help. Whether or not he actually ever goes to a doctor is doubtful, and I don't follow up on my threat after all, not having the stomach for it.

A few months later, my father is given an ultimatum at work when told that the company will pay for him to get some help with his problems. I can only speculate that he had been missing work, showing up late, and/or employing even less restraint than is his custom when voicing opinions.

My father's response to his boss: "I don't need help. You do." He's fired.

I come upon a Spanish artist unfamiliar to me: Remedios Varo. Known as a para surrealist and anarchist, she painted a compelling female figure in a 1961 work called "Mujer

Saliendo del Psicoamalista" ("Woman Coming out of ᴜ Psychoanalyst's"). Estella Lauter, in *Women as Mythmakers: Poetry and Visual Art by Twentieth-Century Women,* describes the painting this way:

> Wearing a green cloak, the veiled woman holds her father's head by the beard, ready to drop it into a well... . Her vision has enabled her to discard the head, embodiment of everything threatening, along with a clock, a key, and a pacifier, which Varo called "psychological waste." Far from achieving atonement with the father, the woman must dispose of his head and assume the ultimate task of creation, resurrection of nature, by herself... .

Varo's woman invades my psyche. Though I have no green cloak or veil, my father no beard, in his role as *father*, mine is expunged.

You do not do...So daddy, I'm finally through.
--Sylvia Plath

STRIVING

And how am I to face the odds
Of man's bedevilment and God's?
I, a stranger and afraid
In a world I never made.
They will be master, right or wrong;
Though both are foolish, both are strong.
    --A.E. Housman,
        "The Laws of God, The Laws of Man"

From these A. E. Housman's lines, Baroness Wootton of Abinger took the words "in a world I never made" for her 1967 book, subtitled *Autobiographical Reflections*. Born Barbara Adam, in Britain, she married John Wootton in 1917; he died weeks later in World War I. Adam, an outstanding intellectual, having studied classics and economics at Cambridge, became the first woman ever to sit in the House of Lords, and received thirteen honorary degrees, including a doctorate from Cambridge. During World War II, she was a conscientious objector, though she was not liable for military service, and in the 1930s, she became a leader in international movements for peace and human rights. A May 1970 entry in my quote book comes from Baroness Wootton:

> It is part of the basic difficulty of communication between individuals. I wonder the human race has

survived at all when you think of the appalling difficulty of two people trying to live together; and the survival of the human race is based on that. The problem is the fundamental loneliness of the individual, from which there is no escape.

Following this entry in my book is a passage from George Eliot's 1859 novel, *Adam Bede*:

> These fellow-mortals, every one, must be accepted as they are: you can neither straighten their noses, nor brighten their wit, nor rectify their dispositions; and it is these people—amongst whom your life is passed—that it is needful you should tolerate, pity, and love: it is these more or less ugly, stupid, inconsistent people, whose movements of goodness you should be able to admire, for whom you should cherish all possible hopes, all possible patience.

Lessons for me, these quotes. I certainly concede the loneliness of the individual, and I endeavor to accept people as they are..., but I have to acknowledge my limitations when it comes to tolerance, pity and love. Without belaboring various political issues, I will simply say that it seems wrong to me to legislate from religious beliefs that infringe upon religious freedom and the American declaration of an individual's right to pursuit of life, liberty, and happiness. If we are to live with freedom, in a society of various belief systems—salad bowl, not melting pot—we must accede to diverse values in order to assure quality life for all. I don't *tolerate* people who clearly demonstrate bigotry and execute deeds of persecution. I do not *love* them. I find them repugnant, avoid them. Powerless though I am to change their minds and actions, it's not for me to take up arms against them, literally or figuratively. My modus operandi becomes, then, *limited engagement* with many of the world's people and their mores, always cognizant of my good fortune, especially as a woman, in being able to keep my limits, living quietly, separately, peacefully, with no expectation that the world at large will ever fit my paradigm for truly *civilized* existence.

I live and do what I have to do to stay in the world, obey laws whether or not I view them as right-good-rational, wait for the end of my unrequested tenure on a planet poised, more than likely, given the violent wars that persist and the planetary destruction resulting in global warming, on the cliff's edge of obliteration. I am as happy, I think, as it is possible to be, for such a one–strange, a stranger, sometimes afraid, in a world I <u>never</u> would have made, a sentiment included in yet another poem, "In Vietnam" by Pablo Neruda:

> And who made war?
> It's been pounding since the day before yesterday.
> I'm afraid.
> It pounds like a stone
> against the wall,
> like thunder with blood,
> like a dying mountain.
> This is a world
> I didn't make.

I live, striving always to withstand men's bedevilment, believing there is no God or gods.

> 'Now what's your point of view?' she asked of her aunt.... 'When I criticize I have mine; it's thoroughly American.'
>
> 'My dear young lady,' said Mrs. Touchett, 'there are as many points of view in the world as there are people of sense to take them. You may say that doesn't make them very numerous! American? Never in the world; that's shockingly narrow. My point of view, thank God, is personal!'
> --Henry James, *The Portrait of a Lady*

In 1973, I graduate from Rutgers University, then visit India again before being hired as an assistant buyer in the china department of a large New Jersey store. Three weeks and I never learn a thing, my vision of going to Europe on a buying trip fading fast. I direct customers to requested patterns, handle their purchases: I'm a sales clerk. Having met a few other women during lunch hours, I find out that the department buyer, a late-middle-aged man, is known to be a misogynist who never teaches young women anything. Dead-end job. I don't like it; I don't like him.

Taking my grievances to the vice president who hired me, I plead for a change. Affable, he re-assigns me to notions: land of buttons, needles, thread, and, strangely, I'd say, bras and girdles. The buyer there, a youngish woman, immediately goes on vacation, and I now help women, mostly mature, find and buy undergarments of suitable size. Sales clerk again. I realize two things: I'm unenthusiastic about girdles; I have a growing distaste for working in a huge place of merchandise, a constant reminder of materialism and shopping addiction. I don't like it.

Another three weeks pass as I learn next to nothing about buying. Back to the VP. This time I get a gentle lecture on how he had to *work his way up* twenty years ago, culminating in an offer to place me in the advertising department. My sources inform me that the director there is of the same ilk as the china guy; a job there would be an even deader end than dinnerware. Facing the VP one more time, I resign. He's sorry, he says, and adds, as if it's of any import, that he's never been more impressed by anyone he's interviewed. Well, I conclude, if I'm so impressive I definitely don't need to work as a sales clerk. After all, that's what I did as a sixteen-year-old high school student.

After leaving girdle-land, I quickly find a new job at a small agency; I'm an insurance clerk now. Founded by a father, taken over by his son, the agency was built up by the former, and the latter, I'm told by female cohorts, is doing a decent job of nudging it into decline. My duties include typing auto insurance invoices and envelopes, which I address *Mr. and Ms.* The boss notices some outgoing mail and soon I'm called into his office for instruction on his preferred method of addressing insureds.

"I know that *Ms.* is being used, but I just like the standard *Mrs.*, so please type the envelopes using that. Call me old-fashioned... ." His smile is slight, his sentence unfinished.

I comply, but type *Mrs. and Mr.*, a reversal of honorifics he never detects.

Christmas time comes and I'm enjoined to help decorate a tree for the office. I decline. Called into the inner chamber again, I say the task was not included in any job description I saw. I know I'm cantankerous, but I dislike the exploitation of underlings–*women*–in small offices.

"Paul does anything I ask him to do," the boss says. "You know, if you were in the army, you'd follow orders. That's just the way it is."

Paul, number two in command, a lazy guy whose shirt cuffs always look dirty, is prone to making clerical errors, and is a sycophant.

"I'm not in an army, would never join one," I declare. "I didn't expect an insurance agency to be run like a military operation." I walk out of the office.

Strangely enough, I'm not fired. So I hang on for a few more months, quitting the job just before I move to London, beginning to understand that nine-to-five and subjection to a boss of any male stripe is not for me.

LONDON

By June 1974, I move to London for my husband's work assignment, which is to last three or four months. Ten days before leaving, we had moved from our two-bedroom house in New Jersey to a three-bedroom duplex, and I had been excited since I was claiming the third bedroom to use as a study, where I'd write more poetry. I immediately set up the room–desk, typewriter, books–letting packed boxes strewn through all the other rooms just sit. We had moved in on a Saturday, and on Monday Gautam called from his office:
"Don't unpack, we're going to London."
"What?!"
One week later we flew into Heathrow.
When I recall the stay in London, I think first of our landlord. After a quick search for housing, a place where we could sign just a short lease since my husband's work assignment was brief, we found the furnished Kensington flat owned by Chelow. I can't say what his first name was, don't even know if I ever heard it. We moved in on a weekend, and, on Monday, Gautam flew to Bordeaux, France, on business for a two-week stay.
My daughter and I were settling in during the first week, seeing what it was like to be somewhere with no TV, no radio, no relatives or friends, and one shared umbrella for walking the streets during pretty much non-stop drizzle or full rain. During this lonely period, we explored as much as we could, going up and down Kensington High Street,

driving down to Knightsbridge and Chelsea, checking out shops, grocery stores, Kensington Gardens, Hyde Park, realizing what a great location we were to live in. A couple of days into the week, the phone rang, and I answered, hearing a man's voice.

"This is Chelow. Just checking to see if there's anything you need. Towels, sheets, kitchen stuff. Anything I can do for you?"

I told him no, that the flat was well-furnished, and we were fine.

Friday came and my daughter and I flew to Bordeaux to stay with Gautam on the weekend, returning to spend one more week alone before he rejoined us. On Tuesday, the phone rang for a second time, no one having called since Chelow had checked up on us, since we knew no one in London.

"Chelow here. How're you doing? Are you seeing a lot of London?"

I told him that I'd been in France for a few days visiting my husband who was there on business and would return at the end of the week.

"Do you ever get to the West End…"

I didn't even know where or what the West End was.

"…Mayfair? I thought maybe we could have lunch some time."

Without hesitation I said, "When men like you ask women like me to lunch, they usually want something more than lunch."

I know now that my phrasing wasn't quite right; I shouldn't have said "women like me." It led straight to his, surprising, I thought, response.

"Are you a lesbian?"

"NO!" I replied, puzzled at the time why he would have asked me that. It was only later, on reflection, that I decided I had left myself open to such a question. And yet, Chelow knew I was married. To a man. Did he think that, if I was straight, regardless of having a husband, I might be interested in having sex with him? And if I wasn't interested, did it follow that I was not straight? After all, he didn't discount my statement, which implied an acquiescence with my reasoning that more than lunch was in the offing. In any event, not only did we have no sex, we did not break lunch bread together either. Not that age differences have ever mattered much to me, but he looked old enough to be my grandfather.

During our London stay, which stretched into an almost year-long period, I was free to roam around; I didn't have a job.

Gautam went to his office each morning, and at summer's end my daughter went off to a private school paid for by the company, a van providing back-and-forth, door-to-door transportation. I learned how to best negotiate the city, using the underground for certain destinations, the bus for others, and our rental car for places where I could easily park. Since British Airways had lost my suitcase on our short return flight from France, I had a little replacement money for lost articles and therefore a good excuse to shop. I made my way not only to the High Street department stores in my neighborhood, Barker's and Biba's, but Selfridge's on Oxford Street, Harrod's in Knightsbridge, and Peter Jones in Chelsea. When it came time to consider a new outfit for the company Christmas dinner dance, then, I was familiar with these stores. But suddenly I had a harebrained idea. Why not buy a men's suit to wear?

Devotee of the unconventional, I liked the idea of being the only Exxon-wife dressed in tweeds with a vest. But after searching and searching through several haberdasheries, I had to conclude that my body style, rather wide-hipped, though I was slim enough then, wasn't made for men's pants, and I had no patience for having anything altered, never wanting to pay that much attention to clothing. I had to settle, instead, for a long black skirt, black blouse with a red rose appliqué, black lace shawl, and some very clunky black platform shoes, popular then, whose heels, though rather high, did not match those of stilettos I see in the 21st century, when I would have expected women to be evolved enough to prefer the comfort of normal walking to hobbling. Looking not quite as eccentric as I would have liked, I thought I still appeared a bit irregular.

While in London, I played the tourist to some extent, visiting Buckingham Palace, Tower of London, Big Ben, Piccadilly Circus, etc., but what I most enjoyed was just living there in my footloose fashion, rambling around, taking classes in handwriting analysis, psycho-cybernetics, yoga, and ballet, going to the theater occasionally, seeing musicals like *Billy*, a guy who daydreams and lies about his life; *John, Paul, George, Ringo, and Bert,* based on the story of the Beatles; and *The Wombles*, adapted from the children's series by a British woman, Elisabeth Beresford. Ahead of her time, Beresford incorporated a strong re-cycling theme in her works, and the Wombles, furry fictional, personified creatures, had a motto: "Make good use of bad rubbish." I applaud and have employed that practice, often in metaphoric ways.

It turned out that the year 1974 was deadly for London, the IRA bombing several places. In June, there was the House of Parliament, eleven people injured. In July an explosion at the Tower of London killed one person and injured forty-one others, including eight children, the blast leaving many people with badly damaged or lost limbs and serious facial injuries. October saw a bomb exploded at a London club for retired military officers, and, in December, the home of Conservative leader Edward Heath was bombed, though he was unharmed. These events were startling to me since they happened years before the U.S. experienced its Oklahoma City bombing; the now-numerous mass murders in public places; and 9-11.

The year before going to London, I had taken a class in British Romantic poetry, so, when I travel to England's Lake District, to visit Wordsworth's Dove Cottage, the poet's Highland lass "leaping and singing by herself" comes to mind. I have held close the memory of "The Solitary Reaper," a short poem that my professor touted as an essential Wordsworth work. I stand in front of the cottage, where William lived with Dorothy, his "dear, dear Sister," his "dearest Friend," as she is referred to in his famous "Tintern Abbey" poem. The self-deprecating Dorothy detested the idea of setting herself up as an author, as she conceded in her journal, so William was beneficiary of her close observations of nature and he freely borrowed images for use in his poetry. Dorothy's journal entry of April 5, 1802:

> ...I never saw daffodils so beautiful they grew among the mossy stones...some rested their heads upon these stones as on a pillow for weariness & the rest tossed & reeled & danced & seemed as if they verily laughed with the wind that blew upon them over the Lake.

Hence, William's famous "I Wandered Lonely as a Cloud," which has the noted daffodils "fluttering and dancing in the breeze, tossing their heads in sprightly dance."

A solitary reaper, I sing to myself, reaping knowledge of *a world,* to echo Housman once again, *I never made.* A world where revolution, like the French one embraced by Wordsworth, Coleridge, Shelley, and Byron, never quite achieves its ends, but in a multitude of ways, in a multitude of places, societies revert to their great inequities. Wordsworth himself lost trust in social reform as an outcome of the French Revolution when the reign of terror, marked by mass guillotine executions, set in. The world, he described in "Tintern Abbey," had a "heavy and weary weight," the world was "unintelligible." That was in 1798. (What is it now, more than two hundred years later? Unintelligible, I say.)

My mind's a *mansion for all lovely forms,* as Wordsworth wrote, my memory, *a dwelling place for all sweet sounds and harmonies.*

Dove Cottage; a walk with Gautam and Tanya through Grasmere in the rain; reading Wordsworth poems in this place of woodlands; pastures with grazing sheep; valleys, lakes, and fells—these are the lovely forms of memory in my mansion mind. But that dwelling has its dungeon, repository of grisly forms. Thirty-six years after my visit to the bucolic Lake District, a bloodbath took place there, a rampage by a cab driver who began his killing spree by shooting his twin brother eleven times. Twelve people shot and killed, all told, twenty-five wounded. This is part of, in that sweet Wordsworthian language, the *still, sad music of humanity*, and, indeed, has *ample power to chasten and subdue*.

Westminster Abbey. I try to be in awe as I approach the Poet's Corner with its memorials to the Romantic poets I studied—Wordsworth, Coleridge, Byron, Shelley, Keats—as well as to Shakespeare, T. S. Eliot, Gerard Manley Hopkins, and Ted Hughes. No women poets are buried there, though there are eight commemorated: the Bronte sisters, Fanny Burney, Elizabeth Barrett Browning, George Eliot, Elizabeth Gaskell, and Jane Austen. Whatever awe I feel standing here in this hallowed gothic church, traditional place of coronation and burial, is for the dismissal or denigration of half the human race, women, by the other half. Men. I feel, too, a kind of awe of myself, as a woman who has never had her heart broken by a man, that tough, sinewy muscle of mine impervious to any Cupid-generated slings and arrows, pumping blood just for me, keeping me in this baffling world.

England was lovely. I recognized and respected the beauty and tradition of buildings, bridges, gardens, but could not forget the bloody history of its *royal* family kings and queens: murder, theft, deceit, slave-trade, war mongering, profiteering, imperialism, and civil oppression. Just like assorted detestable enterprises of countless countries, through hundreds and hundreds of years. England had its infamous Richard (the Third), and the U.S. had its devious Richard (Nixon), whose resignation speech we listened to during our time in London. And then there is that other dishonorable Richard: my own father.

HOW TO LIVE AND WRITE

When English settlers arrive in the "new world" with a vision of owning land, they discover that from the Native American perspective land is communal space and impossible to own. Conflicts begin...

Hin-mah-too-yah-lat-kekt, or Chief Joseph, of the Nez Perce people, faced with settlement by whites of tribal lands in Oregon, led his followers to Canada in an attempt to escape. His father Tuekakas, Chief Joseph the Elder, one of the early Nez Perce leaders converted to Christianity, hence the name Joseph, had established peace with the whites, forging a treaty in 1855 that created a new "reservation" for his people. But peace was fragile, tensions mounted, and eventually Chief Joseph the Younger attempted his retreat, a 1400-mile, four-month march, considered one of the most remarkable retreats in military history.

In 1877, forty miles from his Canada destination, the chief and his people, just 87 left from 700, were exhausted. Chief Joseph famously stated:

> "I am tired of fighting... . Hear me, my chiefs, I am tired. My heart is sick and sad. From where the sun now stands, I will fight no more forever," Chief Joseph said in his surrender speech. It was cold, the people had no blankets, no food. Some had run away, many had died.

According to Jeffrey Ostler in "Genocide and American Indian History,"

> Did the actions and policies of Europeans and U.S. Americans toward Indians qualify as *genocide* or not? However one answers the question, it is true that settlers unleashed massively destructive forces on Native peoples and communities, including violence resulting directly from settler expansion, intertribal violence (frequently aggravated by colonial intrusions), enslavement, disease, alcohol, loss of land and resources, forced removals, and assaults on tribal religion, culture, and language. The configuration and impact of these forces varied considerably in different times and places, according to the goals of particular colonial projects and the capacities of colonial societies and institutions to pursue them. The capacity of Native people and communities to directly resist, blunt, or evade colonial invasions proved equally important.

Is there any land I could live in where my "fathers" had not died...in battle?

Not as long as *dulce et decorum est pro patria mori* rules men's consciousness, termed an "old lie" by World War I poet Wilfred Owen, killed in action at age twenty-five, but not before he wrote of the horrors of trench and gas warfare:

> If in some smothering dreams, you too could pace
> Behind the wagon that we flung him in,
> And watch the white eyes writhing in his face,
> His hanging face, like a devil's sick of sin;
> If you could hear, at every jolt, the blood
> Come gargling from the froth-corrupted lungs,
> Obscene as cancer, bitter as the cud
> Of vile, incurable sores...
> My friend, you would not tell with such high zest
> To children ardent for some desperate glory,
> The old Lie: *Dulce et decorum est*
> *Pro patria mori.*

Sweet and right to die for your country? Fight no more, forever, when fighting's so sweet? The human male, as the gender has evolved, will always love war. Land, country, my country, any country: always a place where fathers kill...and fathers, mothers, children die, as they are currently doing in Ukraine, thanks to Russia.

From my Statement of Intent, in application for the University of Houston's 2003 Krakow Poetry Seminar fellowship:

> I grapple with the issue of how to live and write as a poet in an increasingly politicized and violence-prone environment, how to indulge the need for solitude, beauty, art, and at the same time play a civic role. Is it possible to privilege the part of self poet Adam Zagajewski refers to as "rather anarchic," the self that has no interest in politics, but loves poetry and music? The question he poses in the preface to his *Solidarity, Solitude* is how to live with "contradictory egos"–civic, poetic, and metaphysical... .
>
> To be any part, however small, of the current global protest against war, is to be involved in a political movement, and from my perspective it is impossible not to protest. The question I raise is how anyone on the planet cannot speak out against human-on-human violence that could escalate, with our available war machinery, to annihilation of the entire race... .
>
> I am keenly interested in possible dialogues about how Polish poets have resolved the universal dilemma, those who have contemplated egos through the history of Poland's political struggles.
>
> I would also like to explore the issue of silence–poetic and political, chosen and enforced–
> its power, its uses, its effects. Wisława Szymborska's poem, "The Silence of Plants," concludes with the

lines, "Talking with you is essential and impossible. / Urgent in this hurried life / and postponed to never." Though she speaks throughout the poem of plants, and her "one-sided acquaintance" with them–she knows their names, they don't know hers–I read that urgency and impossibility of communication as the human-to-human sort, as well. Her lines "But how to answer unasked questions, / while being furthermore a being so totally / a nobody to you," speaks, perhaps, of the frustration a poet's civic ego has in the attempt to say something through poetry that can be heard by those who have not requested poetry. Czeslaw Milosz's poem "Zone of Silence" refers to silence kept when there is "a truth too cruel for the human heart," and I wonder how one knows which truth is that cruel... .

My application approved, I was one of ten recipients of a fellowship that paid for air travel, food and week-long lodging in July 2003.

My responsibility was to present and lead a discussion with another student in the seminar room of Jagiellonian University, at a table of students and established poets, some of whom were Pulitzer and Nobel Prize winners. Our topic was "Aesthetics of Disgust," which we initiated from *The Anatomy of Disgust* by William Miller, a book whose title, the author has said, is a play on Robert Burton's 17th-century classic *The Anatomy of Melancholy*, an examination of human emotion. Miller's focus is the function of disgust in human life, which he views as a kind of protection, something that insulates us from anything offensive, disgust serving an important role in our complex human emotional and social makeup.

Determining how a poet might create out of a profound feeling of disgust, what type of poem would emerge (the aesthetics of disgust), was a task I found compelling. Looking at some contemporary Polish poetry I came upon the following, from "Songs of a Wanderer" by Aleksander Wat:

>   Disgusted by everything alive I withdrew

>   into the stone world; here
> I thought, liberated, I would observe from
>   above, but without pride, those things
>   tangled in chaos.
> With the eyes of a stone, myself a stone
>   Among stones, and like them
>   sensitive,
> pulsating to the turning of the sun.
>   Retreating into the depth of myself,
>   a stone,
> motionless, silent; growing cold...

This long poem, in eleven sections, speaks of the heart of a stone, the dreams of a stone, the thought of a stone, asks what riches are to the stone. In section two, the poem reiterates: "disgusted with the world of the living, its beauty turned toward death, decaying.../ I fled into the stone world.../ my eyes, not yet stony but no longer human." The stone itself, the *thought* of which the poem's speaker says he wants to *touch,* might die of disgust because of his *coarse, bulbous fingers, the fingers of a usurper*. Human fingers.

Man, Wat says in another poem, *exhales an abominable smell*; he *provokes disgust and fear*. Better to live as a mouse than a man, is the implication in "To Be a Mouse." But a field mouse, or garden mouse, he adds, because of the pungent smell of the man in a house.

Hungarian writer Ernő Szép, author of a memoir, *The Smell of Humans*, details a forced march during the Nazi takeover of Hungary. The Jewish people rounded up had to endure the march, rancid and burnt food, and the misery of grueling work and lack of sleep. Szép was among those who suffered:

> Again we positioned ourselves along the side wall, where I had left my blanket and knap-sack. We sat for a while, thinking with dismay about having to sleep on that cold brick floor again. The straw had a nauseating smell. Fresh straw has a pleasant scent, but this was tired old straw. I remembered this miserable straw smell from my student years; it was what my straw mattresses used to exhale back then.

The aesthetics of disgust presupposes specific detail, especially involved with discomfort, nauseating *smell* being one exact component of discomfort.

Tadeusz Borowski, the Polish writer who, having survived Auschwitz and Dachau, killed himself in 1951, published a book of stories, *This Way for the Gas, Ladies and Gentlemen* (its American title, though it appeared in the Polish as *Farewell to Maria*). As a depiction of disgust, the description in one story, titled "A True Story," carries Szep's nauseating detail even further:

> I felt certain I was going to die. I lay on a bare straw mattress under a blanket that stank of the dried-up excrement and pus of my predecessors. I was so weak I could not even scratch myself or chase away the fleas. Enormous bedsores covered my hips, buttocks, and shoulders. My skin, stretched tightly over the bones, felt red and hot... . Disgusted by my own body, I found relief in listening to the groans of others.

The aesthetics of disgust includes the use of dramatization and dialogue to enhance description.

This last 3-line stanza of Aleksander Wat's "From Persian Parables" sums up my reaction to our ever-warring world:

> Nothing is ever over
> –the helmsman's voice was hollow–
> and there is no bottom to evil.

The answer to how can we cope with this evil? Wat answers in "Before Brueghel the Elder,"

> Work is a blessing.
> ...
> How else could we deal with the lava of fratricidal
>   love toward our fellow men?
> With those storms of extermination of all by all?

> With brutality that has no bottom, no measure?...
> ...
> Work is our rescue.

The aesthetics of disgust, then, can include imagery of being other than human: stone. It can include description of how to carry on in the world whose brutality has no bottom: work.

A poem by Zbigniew Herbert describes the pebble as "a perfect creature":

> ...filled exactly
> with a pebbly meaning
>
> with a scent which does not remind one of anything
> does not frighten anything away does not arouse desire
>
> its ardour and coldness
> are just and full of dignity

And Charles Simic's poem "Stone" suggests that by going into a stone you become one:

> Go inside a stone
> That would be my way.
> Let somebody else become a dove
> Or gnash with a tiger's tooth.
> I am happy to be a stone.

If a dove symbolizes peace and a tiger's tooth violence, stone is the neutral figure, perhaps beyond peace and violence, beyond good and evil. To be stone is to withdraw, an idea that goes back to Nietzsche's *looking away*, his *only negation*.

To be in the heart of a stone—how much I desired this! Wat wrote. I sometimes feel the same desire, but if I cannot be a stone in this space/time, I can carry light and silence. Countervailing violence, which will never be over in this current lifetime of mine, I'll look, like Nietzsche, away, privileging my poetic/metaphysical ego over the civic one that is incurably powerless and despondent. At the same time, I commend those indefatigable workers for peace and justice, hoping their optimism and visions triumph over my gloom, if only in some small way. I can simply carry light and silence, as Anna Swir wrote:

> Whether in daytime or in nighttime
> I always carry inside
> a light.
> In the middle of noise and turmoil
> I carry silence.
> Always
> I carry light and silence.

Joy, Power, Revenge

> "One reason writers write is out of revenge. Life hurts; certain ideas and experiences hurt; one wants to clarify, to set out illuminations, to replay the old bad scenes and get the Treppenworte said–the words one didn't have the strength or ripeness to say when those words were necessary for one's dignity or survival."
> --Cynthia Ozick

> Is there then a world
> where I rule absolutely on fate?
> A time I bind with chains of signs?
> An existence become endless at my bidding?
>
> The joy of writing.
> The power of preserving.
> Revenge of a mortal hand.
> --Wisława Szymborska

Reveling in revenge, however idiosyncratic mine may be, I derive great joy from writing: holding a pen; tapping a key; playing freely in the field of language as I choose, making-breaking words; setting out my truths with my mortal hand.

Personal power will always be incomplete, imperfect, subject to interpretation and to change, somewhat dependent on external conditions. As long as I am in a dimension dominated by rulers, too often kakistocratical, my power will always be limited, but there are those ancillary powers I can employ in fairly good measure: power to deliberate, refuse, reject, invert, not buy; power to not be ruled by feeling or intellect alone; and the power to not be a self-sacrificing, *nice* female.

Clearly, I have good fortune, especially considering I'm confined in the gender-box tagged *female,* however much I redefine, because if I stay put where I am, it's unlikely I'll be stoned. I have, too, good sense. So as long as I lock my doors and set the alarm; refrain from walking about alone, anywhere, ever, at night; limit my engagement—nay, *refuse* to engage—with men who have the greatest potential for aggression and violence (though who they all are, I can never be sure); carry mace, pepper spray, and/or a taser; make sure my peripheral vision is acute and my level of trust nil; perfect my talent for looking over my shoulder; and hope my luck doesn't run out . . . I just might avoid rape, kidnapping, torture, and murder. This vigilance, then, is an essential component of my system of living.

"I must create a system or be enslaved by another man's," wrote William Blake. I adjust his statement for myself, omitting the *nother.*

Human existence must be a kind of error.
                    --Arthur Schopenhauer

We can only begin to live when we conceive life as tragedy.
                    --William Butler Yeats

Perhaps someday...I will see the other side of this monumental grotesque joke.

And then I'll laugh. And then I'll know what life is.
--Sylvia Plath

Error, Tragedy, Joke
I could have signed on to all of these in 1964. Question to self, post-deathfailure: if living well is the best revenge for having to live, then what is the *well*? I was not capable of answering, much less creating a blueprint for living back then; but now, on reflection, I analyze what has happened in *being* and *doing* through the years since my personal error began and see how a strategy evolved.

As an atheistic, solipsistic quester, I couldn't look for inspiration or consolation from the thought of a heavenly afterlife, or from any of the other Errors (aka humans) running around during my tenure on Earth. So what was I to do? To nutshell it, I embraced non-conformity and hedonism, which meant I would always create and follow my own path, to the extent that it was possible, and repudiate the various prescriptive norms of society that didn't suit me, discovering/originating what would give me satisfaction. The evolution of this approach has equipped me with most everything I might need to maximize pleasure, minimize pain (though even the fine-honing of my techniques has not made the enterprise foolproof).

Two primary precepts form the bedrock of my living-system: 1. get needs, desires, and the necessary labor to fulfill them in line with willingness, ability, focus, and energy; 2. find an authenticity of being that results in balanced associations. The first is largely about achievement and materialism, the second, social intercourse, and the two are interrelated. Hence, my limited engagement with the World and my fellow Errors.

I have made it my business to be somewhat removed from conspicuous consumption based on acquiring status-symbol goods, so that at the advanced stage of my life what I own has been thoughtfully acquired or bestowed upon me. In my two-week, 1965 rat-trap apartment I had a bed, a chair, a lamp, a couple of pots, a couple of dishes and utensils. Not much else, apart from clothes. No knick-knacks, no TV, no table, no appliances, no potted plants, and nothing at all with a designer label. I was satisfied with my measure of rejection of the material. I've moved away from that position since I'm compelled to keep almost everything anyone has given me, wanting to honor, use, display all gifts in deference to the givers. Without a modicum of interest in labels or trends, however, I accumulate on my own only what pleases me aesthetically, what provides comfort, and what increases my library of books and fountain pen collection.

As for balanced associations, I've taken care to discern, and have also had good fortune, encountering, becoming closely connected to or intimately involved with, only good quality people with whom it is easy to be in balance. Very little quarreling, no drama, much serenity.

Maintaining a reverence for language, with all its imperfections and limitations, I remain in love with, committed to, words, and to books, pens and now, in our technologically advanced era, my laptop. What I can do is be and write and wait, kill time until time kills me. And while I *am*, I can enjoy it all as much as possible, especially on days when I don't read or watch the news.

...we grow slack of feature in our melancholy,
and the blue which marks the change
is heavy, thick as ooze...
--William Gass,
On Being Blue: A Philosophical Inquiry

While I was tying myself into life, intent on *being*, intrigued by the various ways of *doing,* the blue membrane that seemed to ring me thickened, until it seemed like a placental home, I the abiding fetus being fed on blue. As I moved forward, yet another human bound in living, I found antidotes for blues malefic, pleasure in some blues agreeable. Through *blue funk* times, I was capable of savoring blue sky, sea, ink; a bright blue shirt, soft blue sweater; a Siamese fighting fish I bought when I was forty-four; a vivid damselfly on a pond; brilliant eyes–my grandmother's. On the way, though, to a homeostatic existence, I had my falterings and at times wondered who this person was, the *me* who made friends, found some lovers, married, had daughters, worked and moved through days and nights in a customary way, kept reading, kept thinking, knew myself entirely and not at all. There were, and still are, those slightly more than split seconds when I am divorced from *I*, as though watching self as someone foreign. Endlessly I rehearsed basic questions: why am I here; what is this *here*; is the state of the human, in particular, *man*, the best that could have developed; was it inevitable that man drug himself, rape, torture, murder, wage war? Will my death end all or will I reincarnate; if so, in human form, on this same planet? Or would the planet be obliterated by men before I could become again, maybe, *flesh*? Could I manifest on another planet, in another galaxy? What kind of form would that be? Or is the end of my present body and consciousness meant to disallow any other, anytime, anywhere? Let that be so, I often mused.

As I grew cognizant of the range of men's atrocities, I developed a horror that increasingly intensified. During my high school years William Shirer's *The Rise and Fall of the Third Reich* was published, and finding it in our living room, my father having brought it from the library, I began to read. A fat book could always lure me back then–like Michener's *Hawaii*, a thousand plus pages, which I had recently read– but when I got to the description of Nazi officers throwing babies into the air and shooting them down, I stopped reading, never finished the book. No further information could penetrate my psyche as deeply as that detail. As a child I had experienced fear of a boy, which deeply affected me, but I mark the Nazi learning moment as the start of my abhorrence of violence, and an understanding of its enormity.

The little neighborhood boy Jerry terrorized me. He had a missing arm but in his one hand he held the only weapon I suppose he had then, a rock. Waving his single arm, rock in hand, he would jump out from behind a bush as I got off the bus that took me home from school.

> Sad flap   an empty sleeve
> one arm raised
> eyes squinting   mouth taunting

a little boy jumping
out from bushes   shouting
>   *You better look out!*

It's mid-June   a few clusters of lilacs
still sweeten the air
but most have rusted
I rub sweaty palms
in the pockets of my dress
I'm six, a little girl
scared of a boy, a rock
in his one hand
when I get off the bus
panicked   by his threat
I hide my fear, carefully
like I hide the Hershey Kisses
left over from lunch
I stare at the rock and the sleeve
where an arm should be
>   *Yes, I look out...*

I read about the Manhattan Project, research and development to produce the first atomic bomb, and how men at Los Alamos, New Mexico created their *blue glow*, grew sick and died of radiation illness...

>   Blue Glow
>   —sounds like a prom in the 50's
>   low lights   flickers of color from a mirrored ball
>   music yearning smell of clean collars and
>   after-shave
>
>   Blue glow   Omega Site   Pajarito Canyon
>
>   Blue glow   plutonium   beryllium sphere
>
>   *Gamma and neutron rays...*
>   *Eight men rushed out of the laboratory...*
>   *drove themselves to Los Alamos Hospital...*
>   *Doctors watched the steady concurrent rise*
>   *and fall*

of the victims' blood counts...as the radiation ran its course through their bodies.

Victims? Men who worked with deliberation determination   to develop their capacity for
        mass destruction?
  Blue glow   Blue glow   Blue glow

No, I thought so often, living is not a good thing to be doing. Not when death was waiting, threatening, inescapable, possibly violent.

Romanian philosopher E. M. Cioran wrote in *The Trouble with Being Born*, "Not to be born is undoubtedly the best plan of all. Unfortunately, it is within no one's reach." So, living was what I was doing, with never a second suicidal thought after 1964, despite days akin to, at times, Emily Dickinson's "Yesterdays in Pairs":

> The first Day's Night had come—
> And grateful that a thing
> So terrible—had been endured—
> I told my Soul to sing...
> ...And then—a Day as huge
> As Yesterdays in pairs,
> Unrolled its horror in my face—
> Until it blocked my eyes...

I sign on to American psychotherapist, author, atheist, Eric Maisel's 2012 existential program, *Rethinking Depression: How to Shed Mental Health Labels and Create Personal Meaning,* and follow his direction, making meaning as I can:

> The word depression is a corruption of language, and the more society uses it, the further it will push us all toward unhappiness. Pathologizing unhappiness creates unhappiness. Reject the very idea of depression and make meaning instead.

NO ONE CAN BE EXACTLY LIKE YOU

> *To have written an autobiography is already to have made yourself a monster. I know of nothing more difficult than knowing who you are, and then having the courage to share the reasons for the catastrophe of your character with the world. Anyone honestly happy with him [her] self is a fool.*
> *(It is not a good idea to be terminally miserable about yourself either.)*
>
> –William Gass, "The Art of Self"

End of lunch in a Chinese restaurant and here's the customary fortune cookie, one of those without a fortune but, rather, a pronouncement: *No one can be exactly like you.* So I think about who I am and who my *you* might be, i.e., what other people see and assume. I ponder identity and how it's formed, on what it's based.

While I reject the ascendancy of a common construct, sexual/gender identity, I know that the first thing my *you* appears to be is female, and however much I may eschew the reigning gender binary, I won't escape that designation. I can shop in the men's department, buy and wear men's shirts (I do); favor a daily ensemble of T-shirts and jeans (I do); spurn dresses, skirts, lace and ruffles (I do); refuse to display uncovered abdomen or cleavage; adopt a certain male-like assertive presentation of self, but in the end the first thing that anyone would say about me is that I'm a woman (I do wear lipstick). And that's okay with me. So I embrace my strongly female body as well as my less-than-fully-feminine character, and sometimes wear pearls with my denim and men's shirts (and always lipstick).

There are people who now view themselves as constituents of one of the newer categories of sex/gender, such as bigender, cisgender, transgender, intersex, two-spirit, boi, etc. There are those who are heterosexual, homosexual, bisexual, transsexual, and pansexual, i.e., experiencing sexual / romantic / physical / spiritual attractions to all gender types. As one who finds intelligence the most sexually attractive feature, I learned that I'm a *sapiosexual,* or *sapio-bisexual,* but I'm more interested in how to fashion identity apart from/aside from/beyond sex and gender. How I define myself rather than in how strangers on the street see me.

One truth of my own being is grounded in two things: (1) most of my time on this earth has been/is spent *not* participating in sexual activity, and *not* welcoming or permitting penetration (despite a time of premarital and marital sex); (2) I have never felt unconditionally aligned with my assigned gender. In my thinking, then, I invalidate the dictum that *every* personal identity must be constructed, primarily, in the same way, or that a being must take on, and take to heart, whatever label society confers, based on what societal agreement has become.

So I ruminate. What one marker, if it had to be just one, could I attach, contentedly, to myself? What essence is so strong as to be the one of greatest consequence?

Simply happenstance that I begin reading Mary Shelley's now-famous novel in the very city where she created the eponymous character whose nameless creation has been known for almost two centuries now as Frankenstein, popular culture conflating maker and monster. Taking advantage of our proximity to the continent while we live in London, my husband, daughter, and I cross the channel with our rental car in a hovercraft and drive through several European countries. In packing reading material for the trip,

I had included *Frankenstein,* a book I knew of but had never read, unaware that the story's locale was one of our destinations: Geneva, the Alps.

When Lord Byron challenged the group of friends staying at Villa Diodoti on Lake Geneva during the summer of 1816 to write a ghost story, raging storms forcing them to stay indoors, Mary Shelley began her tale. And now, more than a hundred and fifty summers later, here I am in the Frankenstein environs beginning the book known as a landmark work, one prompting innumerable interpretations. Partly because of the extraordinary experience of reading it in plain sight of Mont Blanc—where *power dwells apart in its tranquillity,/ remote, serene, and inaccessible,* as Percy Shelley's poem describes it— *Frankenstein* would become the most significant novel for me.

Fact: a nineteen-year-old girl wrote *Frankenstein.* Fact: the novel's power of endurance and pervasiveness, through literature and pop culture, has been mammoth. Possibility: the name alone may be better known than that of any other book or character in western literature.

I spent a great deal of time re-reading *Frankenstein* during graduate school and thinking about its significance, and after much contemplation came to my own interpretation, subject of a required paper I wrote: the nameless monster whose features his creator said he had *selected* as *beautiful—lustrous black* hair, teeth of *pearly whiteness—*whose initial mutterings were *inarticulate sounds,* was the power and embodiment of the female imagination, thus terrifying to Victor Frankenstein. In his first conversation with the monster, maker Frankenstein acknowledges his anger and hatred:

> ...[the monster] had at first deprived me of utterance, and I recovered only to over whelm him with words expressive of furious detestation and contempt.
> "Devil!" I exclaimed, "do you not fear the fierce vengeance of my arm wreaked on your miserable head? Begone, vile insect! or rather stay, that I may trample you to dust!"

The monster's plea for his creator to make him happy so that he can be *mild and docile* to his *natural lord and king* is futile.

> "Begone! I will not hear you. There can be no community between you and me; we are enemies. Begone, or let us try our strength in a fight, in which one must fall."

This creature, viewed by Frankenstein as hideous, abhorrent, wretched, knows he (she?) has the capability to be good: "I was benevolent; my soul glowed with love and humanity; but am I not alone, miserably alone?" And the creature is, in truth, more powerful than his creator, having been made with superior height and more supple joints.

> "Listen to my tale. When you have heard that, abandon or commiserate me, as you shall judge that I deserve. But hear me. Hear my tale; it is long and strange..."

The creature then tells the tale.

Strange: a word whose synonyms are *unusual, odd, curious, peculiar, funny, bizarre, weird, uncanny, queer*. A word, like orange, that has the *ange* of *anger*. I think I am strange, have anger, am sometimes orange like my mother. And although I've had depression at times, I am now mostly stripeless, however much there is the tiger in me.

What words do we use to describe ourselves? With what descriptors do we create personal identity? What other beings wish to self-create, self-name, unearth a self and bestow a word for it that captures essence? I think the marker I would use for my intrinsic nature would be *quester*. This word for *one who searches* has that letter I've always liked–Q (10-pointer in Scrabble!). I've been that being throughout life, looking first for a beautiful stone; then a beautiful way of living, a way of having contentment; some material thing or just the right word to convey a thought, feeling, idea. I am the consummate quester.

The word partakes of another Q word–*queer*–having the same initial q-u-e, exactly those letters in my name *Jacquelyn*. The multiple uses of *queer* have practically been subsumed through the history of homosexuality, and the word has endured its period of contempt, only to be reclaimed for other uses, like academic, as in "queer studies." A measure of the word's meanings may be imputed to my Quester label. I don't mind. And certainly the verb sense, *to spoil or ruin,* is apt, as well; I am one who means to *queer* the idea of identity formation as the exclusive privilege of society instead of the individual, to *queer* the imperative that identity be dominated by gender.

Coming to terms with the being that one has, however, evolved, however flawed, is not always an agreeable process, but self-acceptance in itself can be gratifying. I believe that anyone who is deeply reflective can never be 100% contented with her (his) essence of being, and so I acknowledge that I remain somewhat discomfited by certain facets of my true character, which I won't dwell on here! The next step, then, is to accept the state of discomfiture; I do, but acceptance of such is imperfect too.

I'm in opposition, I wear opposition like a favorite gown, or robe, cloak, one stitched to accommodate every contour of my self. Its sleeves are buttoned at my wrists, its hem swishes against my ankles when I walk, its neckline circles my underchin. And I feel stunning, stunning in my outfit, fit and fitted out in misfittery for coping with a world not of my making; competent to find, through relentless questing, my idiosyncratic means of contentment.

Call me Ishmael, Melville wrote; call me anything you like, I say. Or no name at all, like Frankenstein's creation, who was known simply as a monster.

A poem I once wrote, "Ode on What I'm Not":

I sing of what I'm not   nor
  wish to be   fun-
damentally I'm no philosopher
no thundrous wisdom here
  clearly do I see
    I'm not a proph-
esier   gloom & doom
  fortune & fame obtain no place
         in   this   space
  where I gam-
bol   psychologist is not the gist
  of my syntonic ego   I've uncovered
    the archeologist is nowhere
near my here & now
  & how I might bloom as a botanist
is subject for only the humorist
  never mistaken for moralist
fabulist   journalist   folklorist
alchemist   physicist   biblicist

One truth found here: I'm not
a true metaphysician or mathematician
My (wo)manifesto
   will lead me to orate with gusto
      & sincerely
   the rhetorician is not nearly
me   You, the universe, all
should see ontologically
     there's no cosmologist
  in me   You can believe
   I will not pose as art
historian   No Breughel brou-
haha of butts & bugles here   a mu-
  sicologist I do not parallel
No reference to the fifth   the ninth   the past-
  orale   appoggiaturas to the es-

>   sence here   Syllogistically it can be shown
>   logician's a position I can't own
>   No magician, still, I have made them all—
>   ists   icians   ologists   et al.
>   entirely disappear...
>   So how do I appear?

???

I'm teaching freshman English composition, give my students a classic assignment: write a descriptive essay about a person, place, or object. The following excerpts are from a four-page paper submitted:

> She looks like she can be between forty and forty-five years of age. She has very few wrinkles.... Her make-up is almost flawless; and if she does have any on at all, it is transparent.... Her dark, golden eyebrows set off her eyes; they're full, but not thick and muddled. They appear to have a perfect arch.... Her eyes are bright blue.... Her lips have an unusual shade of red. Further exploration justifies she has three different shades of lipstick on her miniature lips. It only leads one to believe that she is a very creative woman. Who do you know matches various colors of lipstick to make her own unique shade?...

Here's where it registers—I think my student has written about me! I remember her asking one day what color lipstick I was wearing.

> She tends to smile a lot. Her smile is warm and assuring.... She is standing there wearing a gray shirt, burgundy sweater, gray pants, burgundy socks, and black sandals with two straps neatly crossing for a secure fit. Her accessories are peculiar. She is wearing black and silver earrings that have an unusual shape. They are neither too small, nor too huge. At the top of the earring is a circle encoded with a black, solid filling, and then following the even-cut circle is an odd shape. It closely resembles the shape of a teardrop that looks like it is in the process of falling. On her left ear there is a small, silver loop. It is awkward because the right ear does not have a small silver

loop at all. In the place where there should be a silver loop, there is nothing.

Yeah, it's me. At this point I'm overwhelmed by the detail this assiduous observer has employed…but it goes on and on…description of the rest of my jewelry, my hair, my teeth, my movements, my speech, my hands and their "clean, tidy, short nails."

> Watching her speak in her calm, but strong voice you could recognize that she is very intelligent… . As she speaks quickly, but clearly, her hands move constantly…. She talks with confidence and when she gets excited it can be heard in her voice and seen on her face… .

My mouth twitches, she notes; I lose my train of thought every now and then, but rapidly collect myself. I say, "Okay," frequently. One assumes I do it to reassure my listeners, she has decided.

> She seems to be an incredibly open-minded character, and she is definitely not afraid to express her opinions. She takes criticism better than most individuals.

> …She once said, "I am put on this earth to do this, then die." [I did?!] She is polite, understanding, and respectful, but something about her says that if you cross her there will be hell to pay.   [Astute.] She is a fascinating individual.

Lord, I must be if she has studied me long and hard enough to create this exhaustive profile!

> She seems to be the kind of person that could never be figured out, even if you spent all of your spare time doing so. What leads one to this conclusion about her is the tattoo on her left arm…she does not seem like a tattoo person. She seems to be a self-satisfied person with high standards only set for her.

> [Perceptive, this girl.] She gives her audience the impression that she is an individual who is not concerned with any negative opinions or remarks that could   be

> about her.... She is a leader and demonstrates that women should have pride and confidence in all they do and all they will do. She is unquestionably a woman that has wisdom to share. The woman that has been admired and portrayed throughout this essay is none other than...

And there it is, my very own name. In all my teaching time, this revelation remains the most startling: standing in front of a group of students, class after class, one can never know how closely she is being observed and what conclusions are being drawn. Unless and until someone suddenly has in mind to write it all down.

If I was fascinating to this student, she was, herself, intriguing, because of her scrutiny, her diligence, her indefatigability, and her beauty: she was a young, black woman with blue eyes. Always the dubious one, though, I consider that she might have been simply calculating, thinking that if she wrote about me and was complimentary enough, she might get a good grade. While I'm willing to hold this skepticism in abeyance, I remain more confident about a fifth-grader's sincerity. Beaming, proud of her grasp of the day's topic–simile and metaphor–she reads to the class her description of me, which I treasure as the highest compliment ever paid me:

> "You're like a hamburger with everything on it."

Her stature, her powerful voice, the beads in her dreadlocks, belly in her laugh, seduced me. Her questing mind, tenacious grip on the world, brilliance and unswerving movement to expand her consciousness reeled me in. This is how I described what I first appreciated about the woman I met in 1992. She, too, is *like a hamburger with everything on it.*

When I met Risë, I did something completely out of character for one who practices limited engagement. After leaving the racism-healing workshop we had both attended, I walked up to her and threw my arms around her (never, ever had I done such a thing!).

"You are so beautiful!" I exclaimed. (In retrospect, I couldn't believe I had done that.)

Our friendship developed rapidly, and in 1995 we pledged unending friendship at a bonding ceremony, reading at the event our co-authored "Black Sun Rising," a two-voice performance poem in three parts. It chronicles the developing friendship of two women whose diversities and commonalities have drawn them together and nurtured their mutual affection and commitment to each other. A three-part work, Part I details the beginnings of the friendship and is, overall, playful, intimate, and exploratory. Part II is a collaborative look at the world and how cultures have contributed to divisiveness among people; it is a strong, holding-accountable kind of assessment of things. Part III is an attempt to explore visions for "living a difference in occupied territory," and a reiteration of commitment to change and to love.

At the time of our writing "Black Sun Rising," our respective bios were:

> Risë: a writer with a B.F.A. in drama from Carnegie Mellon, and an ex-Broadway actress holding a Master's degree in political social work from the University of Houston; currently counseling people with sexually transmitted diseases.
>
> Me: a writer with a B.A. and M.A. in English literature, currently working on an M.F.A. in creative writing while teaching through Houston's *Writers in the Schools*.

A program for our bonding ceremony lists the order of events and reads, on the back:

> "We believe that the commitment to love in friendship should be honored and publicly celebrated as joyously as commitment to love in other unions such as marriage. Because we value our three-year-old friendship, we hope to set a new precedent with this friendship bonding ceremony."

We designed, and had made, rings that we placed on each other's fingers as marrying couples usually do. The thick-and-thin of many years gone by, including deaths and moves and aging and such, has not ended the promises we made, among them *to allow no person, place, or thing to separate us*. Nothing has.

I don't call myself a monster, but I embrace the label *mutant*–that being seen as strange, abnormal, or bizarre. And I'm content that no one can be exactly like me, as my fortune cookie pronouncement assured me.

OUT OF BODY, OUT OF MIND

1966. A year when *good* girls still don't have sex until marriage...or pretend they don't. Tell lies about what they are doing, to protect their *good* reputations.

I live with two roommates, Polly and Dana, in a swinging-singles apartment complex near a university. Polly is having sex with Mark, the divorced guy who lives downstairs, spends each evening with him, comes back upstairs at 5:00 a.m. to get ready for work, looks at me sheepishly. *We fell asleep on the sofa watching TV*, she says. And I believe her, almost.

Polly is impregnated by Mark, who doesn't want to marry her. She has an abortion, a backstreet illegal abortion, since women, by virtue of men's legislation, have no reproductive rights in the U.S. and cannot safely end their unwanted pregnancies.

I know nothing about Polly's situation...until Dana tells me she's in the hospital. Her temperature is 106 degrees; she's packed in ice; she almost dies.

Polly survives, but she will never be able to have children. She marries some other guy, and I never see her again.

1972. *The Stepford Wives* is published by novelist Ira Levin. In the fictional town of Stepford, Connecticut, the married men have fawning, submissive, impossibly beautiful wives.

A woman protagonist accuses the men of creating robots out of the town's women.

1980–seven years after the Roe v. Wade landmark decision by the United States Supreme Court on the issue of abortion. I have two children and don't want any more; I'm an advocate of zero population growth. Not trusting that men will maintain the legal status of a woman's reproductive rights (how prescient I was!), I decide I must have permanent protection from unwanted pregnancy. I don't want my husband to have a vasectomy. I want my *own* protection. I order a tubal ligation, and my female gynecologist schedules the procedure, asking no questions. No more pills, condoms, gels, creams, foam, or worry about legal and safe abortion remaining an option. Nothing but freedom for me, and the peace of mind and quality of life that comes with it. I've gone out of my body, the one reproductively serviceable.

1985. Canadian writer Margaret Atwood publishes her dystopian novel, *The Handmaid's Tale*. In it, a totalitarian, theocratic state has replaced the U.S. and because of dangerously low reproduction, handmaids are assigned to bear children for elite couples that have trouble conceiving. I read the novel and think it's not far-fetched.

    A Handmaid named Offred, i.e., *of a man named Fred,* is the novel's central figure. She may leave the home of the Commander and his wife once a day to walk to food markets whose signs are now pictures instead of words, because women are no longer permitted or taught to read. Once a month, Offred must lie on her back and pray that the Commander impregnates her because Handmaids are valued only if their ovaries are viable. Offred can remember the years before when she lived with her husband, had a job and money of her own, and access to knowledge. But all of that is gone. I view *The Handmaid's Tale* as both scathing satire and dire warning.

1989. I'm reading *From Housewife to Heretic*, published by Sonia Johnson in 1981. An ex-Mormon woman self-defined as "a warrior in the time of women warriors" whose "sword is the longing for justice," Johnson was excommunicated by men she calls "stand-ins for God, the god-men of the Mormon church."

This description from the book is apt:

> Everybody born on planet earth since about 2500 B.C. has believed, whether they were religious or not...that God and men are in an Old Boys' Club together...with God as President. And because they are all guys, they have a special understanding... God only has to take one look at them to see that men are superior in every way to the rest of us, because they look like him. So he loves them very much... . He intends them to be the presidents, and prime ministers, the kings of the world. He wants them to be the popes and prophets and priests. He wants them to own all the property and businesses and money, and make all the decisions, and boss everybody else around, meaning women.

I note these words of Johnson in her *Going Out of Our Minds: The Metaphysics of Liberation* (1987): "Since truth is revered in patriarchy, to go out of our minds is to become most truly sane." I go out of my mind, stay there, and stay sane.

2012. The Republican candidate for U.S. president, a Mormon, favors the overturning of Roe v. Wade. There seems to be more sexual activity than ever, and women face the prospect of backstreet abortions once again. In the face of retrograde guys who would outlaw contraception, however, there are alternatives like crocodile dung and beaver testicle tea, though keeping such pets to assure unlimited supplies would probably be illegal as well. Half a squeezed lemon, though, would be an easy thing to come by, to be employed as a diaphragm. Such are the ancient, inferior safeguards that might have to be resurrected to prevent men impregnating women who don't want to have babies.

A quote by another, extremely conservative, Mormon man: "We're giving our freedoms away. The American experiment was about freedom. Freedom to be stupid, freedom to fail, freedom to succeed."

Am I losing my mind? What does freedom mean? How can a man speak of freedom and advocate a totalitarian and theocratic state at the same time, which this guy, and others like him, seem to do? Am I losing my mind? I lost it once by choice; I seem to be losing it all over again.

Is it really 2012? Yes, the 21st century—whatever that means—is well underway. But women, who are graduating from college in greater numbers than men, are more vulnerable than ever, conditioned by the fashion, magazine, and celebrity industries. Mincing around on stilettos; short skirts just barely swishing below their buttocks; breasts bulging, some with implants, from form-fitting, cleavage-showing tops; long hair loose and curly, loose and straight, loose and stringy, women are more sexualized than ever. Violence and sex and violent sex proliferate. "Human trafficking" really means enslavement of women, and children for sex purposes. Patriarchal forces have achieved the remarkable feat of relegating highly educated women to the clutches and churches of men, where they are firmly caught and kept. Kept women, as ever.

2016. An unbelievable election year. I have nothing more to say.

2020, 2021, 2022...what country am I living in?

Boys will be boys...

> 2013 news story: *an 8-year-old boy intentionally shot and killed his 87-year-old grandmother after playing a realistic, violent video game that awards points to the players for killing people.*

Amazed, appalled. That's what I am when I consider certain aspects of *play* and *sport* that have caused pleasure for humans, especially boys and men. And I ask again, was it inevitable that the human male evolve the way it has? Are there other life forms in our universe, or multiverse (if that hypothetical construct actually exists), that behave differently; are not destructive, or self-destructive; whose *play* is harmless; whose *sport* is innocuous; who do not revel in *horror*, like fans of scary movies and haunted houses? It's inconceivable to me that the nature of earthlings represents all life forms, that there isn't some realm populated by peaceful beings.

Well...there is the *bonobo,* once called *pygmy chimpanzee,* an endangered great ape said by primatologist Frans de Waal to be capable of altruism, compassion, empathy, kindness, patience, and sensitivity, whose society is described as a *gynocracy,* that is, one ruled by females. Bonobos seem to prefer sexual contact over violent confrontation with outsiders, *having sex* (apparently a lot of it!) their means of conflict resolution.

Play [noun]: activity engaged in for enjoyment and recreation (*New Oxford American Dictionary*). Men began as boys playing with toy soldiers-guns-rifles, action figures, superheroes. They have now moved to video games that simulate violent actions, including killing. Participants or spectators, they thrill to the sport, the game: football, boxing, hunting, fishing, chess, etc. They bet on outcomes, engage in sustained conversation about which guy, which team of guys, is the best, at killing or refraining from killing, just tackling, punching, besting, always besting. Their play is a kind of war, always.

From internet site http://www.toysoldierco.com:

Just the words 'toy soldiers' can bring a smile to the face of those with a love of history and joy of play.

Whether the affection is for plastic, metal or resin toy soldiers, the passion for these 'little men' is the same.

Play? Passion—for war and killing?

High-profile boy killers: Joshua Carl Jordan Eric Amarjeet Michael Graham Jesse Daniel George Paul Jon Robert Lionel Barry Craig Connor Simon Brandon Edmund Roderick Sam James Nathan Richard Andrew Mitchell Christian Willie Luke Tyler Greg Brian David Dylan Jamie Seth Lyle John Larry Alex Derek Marcelo Ronald William Jeffrey Kipland… .

Sure, there may be girl killers too—but far, far fewer in number.

Men will be Men...

Renowned for pushing their bodies and minds to the limit, training and preparing (with unimaginable intensity), certain men are forever readying themselves for annihilation. Think U.S. Green Berets, British S.A.S or Russian Spetsnaz. Think Little Boy, Fat Man, or any one of these weapons:

> Atomic Annie
> Hybrid Insect MEMS
> The Paris Gun
> Scramjet propulsion X-51A
> WaveRider
> MQ-9 Reaper Drone
> M1 Abrams Tank
> Prompt Global Strike
> PHASR Rifle
> HTV-2 (traveling 20 times the speed of sound)
> AC-130U Spooky
> A-10 Thunderbolt
> The Iron Dome

      The Black Knight
      The Kongsberg NSM
      MAARS Robot
      The Nuclear Bomb
      Laser Avenger
      Railgun
      Chinese Weapons Killer
      XM2010 Enhanced Sniper Rifle
      BioDesign Synthetic Organisms
      IAWS (Individual Airburst Weapon System)
      Dread Silent Weapon System

The *war to end all wars,* WWI, didn't. Nor did WWII.

> The bombing of Dresden in 1945 by Britain's Royal Air Force and the United States Army Air Forces remains a controversial Allied action. The inner city was largely destroyed by 722 RAF and 527 USAAF bombers, which dropped 2431 tons of high explosive bombs and 1475.9 tons of incendiaries. The bombs damaged buildings and exposed their wooden structures; the incendiarites ignited them. Almost all of the ancient city center was destroyed in three waves of attacks. Their combined labors killed 250,000 people in twenty-four hours and destroyed all of Dresden, possibly the world's most beautiful city.
>   –Kurt Vonnegut

So it goes...

In 1989, I unwittingly started an organization: WAVE: Women Against Violence Everywhere. I had one objective: a take-back-the-night march that might be replicated in other cities, creating waves of protest. Through the influence of people I drew to me, my scheme morphed into something ongoing after a city-wide march took place in 1990 at the time of Houston's economic summit. Street corner protests, mini-marches in neighborhoods where violence had occurred, news articles, TV coverage, flyers distributed that twice resulted in the apprehension of rapists...these were WAVE's activities, which culminated in the 1992 Summit on Crimes Against Women, sponsored by the city and its police department. Then I retired, never having wanted to run an organization, since I had a greater interest in writing.

During the time of WAVE, I had started collecting articles on worldwide violent crimes, from which I began crafting poems during a month-long stay at a writers' retreat in the south of France in 2007, titling my collection *Then All Smiles Stopped,* using a line from Robert Browning's famous dramatic monologue, "My Last Duchess."

Browning's poem begins with a hint of what his monologist has done: "That's my last Duchess painted on the wall, / Looking as if she were alive."

Inspired by an actual historical event, the suspicious death of a 16th century Italian Duke's wife of three years, the seventeen-year-old Lucrezia di Cosimo de Medici (possibly poisoned), Browning's poem ultimately underscores the implication of foul play by its principal character, the duke who guides a visitor on a tour of his artwork. Jealousy is evident when the duke says to his guest:

> Oh, sir, she smiled, no doubt,
> Whene'er I passed her; but who passed without
> Much the same smile? This grew; I gave commands;
> Then all smiles stopped together. There she stands [in the painting]
> As if alive... .

The poems I wrote feature atrocities representing eight countries, five continents. I tried to keep language spare, the poems devoid of personal commentary, letting the iniquities speak for themselves. Two examples:

Harmless

The long ordeal of the sisters was made worse because they could find no ally.   USA, 1994

Eyes downcast, stoop-shouldered, handcuffed
he shuffled past his neighbors
Harmless, he looked harmless

Everyone knew
they lived with a monster
three daughters molested and beaten

They were fine
when their father was sober
Many days in a week
he came home drunk
threw the dog against a wall

Police silenced the girls' pleas:
Just disappear on weekends
Go back on Monday when he's sober

Twenty-seven years–
he thought he'd never get caught
People knew
and they ignored it
said the youngest daughter

With the oldest, he fathered two babies
killed both at birth
burying one in the coal bin
one in the yard
Harmless, he looked harmless

They Will Not Stop Us

This practice has been passed down
generation after generation, so it is natural.
Egypt 2007

Seething, the men were seething...
a girl was dead

For centuries the practice persisted–

circumcision by doctor barber
or whoever else in the village
would put a girl to sleep
cut out her clitoris

It assures chastity
prevents homosexuality
preserves family honor
say the imams in their mosques
Genital mutilation is good

The men were seething...
the clinic was closed
a ban on all genital cutting
imposed by the health minister

"Don't criticize the practice
of our fathers, and forefathers.
It is natural to circumcise a daughter.
Even if the state doesn't like it
we will circumcise the girls!
They will not stop us!"
   a man on the street shouts.
"They will not stop us!"

Domination   Torture   Rape   Murder   War   Men.

We will not stop them.

"He, and if there is a God, I am convinced he is a he, because no woman could or would ever fuck things up this badly...," said George Carlin, social critic, actor, author, stand-up comedian.

But it's so good that there are nice guys, plenty of nice guys. That's nice.

The history of meanings for *nice* includes a negative start as *foolish, silly*; stints as *wanton, extravagant, cowardly, slothful, shy* and *reserved*; and the current positives: *fine, pleasant, agreeable, likable, polite, courteous. Nice to meet you*: the (frequent) inauthenticity of this greeting substantiates that *nice* is a wimp of a word.

Nice guy, a common term used to describe a male with friendly personality traits, can be negative as well as positive, since it may mean *unassertive. Nice guy* may refer to honesty, loyalty, romanticism, courtesy, and respect. A Wikipedia entry suggests that when the term is used in a negative context, it's sometimes capitalized and implies a man who does not express his true feelings, is ostensibly friendly but has the unstated aim of romance and sex. In other words, the Nice Guy may very well be devious, and odious.

Like Orthus the mythological dog, Nice Guy is two-headed. Which means he speaks out of two mouths, the equivalent of a real guy speaking out of both sides of his one mouth. He says he values all those good traits like honesty, loyalty, etc., and often claims to be a family man, to value children and their education. But he also reveres tough guys, those who kick ass, and may secretly aspire to do the same. Or not so secretly.

Why are fictional heroes of film and comics called *super*? Meaning *excellent, superb, superlative, first-class, outstanding, marvelous, magnificent, wonderful, splendid, glorious.* Why was the 2010 film called *Kick-Ass* well-received by audiences and critics, despite its profanity and violence? (To cite just one little example…what a plethora, though, there is of such stuff!) To be *super* is to *kick ass,* i.e., be *violent.* Society places value on the super, violent ass-kicker, much more than on the nice (non-violent) guy.

Nice Guys, as they're being upstanding citizens, write, film, enact, time and again, ad nauseam, the violence of killing, fire, explosions, holocausts. And why? Because Nice (film-making) Guys love it, and it makes money; and Nice (film-viewing) Guys love to watch it. And women. Some of those never-nice-in-the-first-place guys love it, too, are sometimes inspired by it. A contemporary tragedy.

Song title, book title, and now a common phrase included in idiom dictionaries, *no more Mr. Nice Guy,* is an apt summation of an attitude too prevalent. Now, if the phrase meant that our shoddy Nice Guys were going to be *no more,* replaced by the genuine article, girls and women would stand to greatly benefit. But sadly it is the mantra of men, many men, a message sent for assurance that the messenger is damned well not going to be *nice* ever again. Nice guys finish last, it's said.

"Nice guys. Finish last," I say, "go on, finish last you Nice Guys. Be bold enough and brave enough to finish last, virility and self-esteem intact."

Really now, who would want to be called *nice*? Women. They have been encouraged to be nice: helpful, charitable, ready to put everyone else's needs, father's, brother's, husband's, children's, community's, before theirs. I quote here contemporary writer Barbara Ehrenreich: "I'm not a nice person." And Margaret Anderson (founder and publisher of the avant-garde literary magazine *The Little Review* 1914-1929): "My unreality is chiefly this: I have never felt much like a human being. It's a splendid feeling." It was said about Anderson that it was surprising to see a coiffure so neat on a "noggin so stormy."

Woman-hating, or *misogyny,* is much more rampant than man-hating, *misandry,* and can be summed up neatly: hatred or dislike of women or girls. It manifests in numerous ways, including sexual discrimination, denigration of women, violence against women, and sexual objectification of women, and can be found within many mythologies of the ancient world as well as various religions. In fact, women endure it every day of their lives, if not the most virulent strains, the comparatively innocuous garden-variety types, like dismissal and exclusion.

Many Western philosophers have been described as misogynistic, and many men have uttered words like *bitch, whore, cunt, slut, douchebag, bimbo, floozy, pig, dog*. But here's a reality, summed up in this quote by writer Margaret Atwood: "Men are afraid that women will laugh at them. Women are afraid that men will kill them."

2023. What horrors are in store for the world now? What will I witness before I leave it? I plan for my limited engagement with the world to include watching less and less of the news, which is anything but new.

And now I *abandon* what cannot be *finished,* according to Leonardo da Vinci and Paul Valery–art and poetry–leaving with one last articulation, interrobanged:

I'm mad about my living

FOOTNOTE

On my foot I write a note
    so it knows where not to go

knows to flee simoom
    find its fettle & thrive

understanding, always
    pogonology & predator

I write it polyglottally
    write by day   deliver nightly

as foot begins to find its play   hop-
    scotching scores & scores

inside its drawing-room   alone

About the Author

Jacquelyn Shah, iconoclast, pacifist holds: A.B. English–Phi Beta Kappa, magna cum laude, Rutgers U; M.A. English, Drew U; M.F.A. and Ph.D.–English literature/creative writing–poetry, U of Houston.

She has received grants from the University of Houston, Houston Arts Alliance, and the Puffin Foundation. Her publications include a chapbook, *small fry*; a full-length book, *What to Do with Red*; and poems in *Rhino, Gyroscope Review, The Texas Review, Vine Leaves* (Australia), *The Lake* (UK), *Plath Profiles, Rushing Thru the Dark,* Autumn 2022, *The Best of Choeofpleirn Press*, Winter 2022, et al. She was *Literal Latté's* 2018 Food Verse Contest winner.

The Kenneth Johnston Nonfiction Book Contest
Judge's Comments

Can a woman be a tour de force? Of course, she can.

Jacquelyn Shah certainly seems to be in her memoir, *Limited Engagement: A Way of Living*.

What begins with a common childhood adventure into the wilderness behind her house becomes Shah's sometimes turbulent voyages to other places and relationships with other people, while trying to navigate the ever-judgmental opinions of her parents. Arching over everything are society's expectations for women, which Shah found limiting, suffocating, and rudely underestimating, seemingly even from the start.

This memoir lulls readers into Shah's experiences by sharing moments from her personal quote journal and letters, only to jolt us back to reality with revelations that changed her life and her outlook on it. Shah does not shy away from the difficult, including her own attempt at suicide, the loss of her virginity, and the sexism she encountered on the job and from her husband's co-workers. This book could just as well be the story of most American women who are passionate about women's rights.

What stood out to me as I read the top manuscripts for the contest is Shah's unmitigated passion for life, language, and peace.

The **Kenneth Johnston Nonfiction Book Award** is an annual creative nonfiction book contest that runs from the first week of September through the end of December.

See www.choeofpleirnpress.com/nonfiction-book-contest for submission guidelines.

The **Jonathan Holden Poetry Chapbook Award** is an annual poetry chapbook competition for poets who have not yet published a chapbook or a full-length collection of poetry. Submissions are accepted from the first of January until the end of April.

See www.choeofpleirnpress.com/poetry-chapbook-contest for submission guidelines.

Choeofpleirn Press publishes four annual literary magazines:
Coneflower Cafe is devoted to fiction, poetry and art.
Glacial Hills Review highlights nonfiction, poetry, and art.
Rushing Thru the Dark features one-act plays, short screenplays, poetry, and art.
The Best of Choeofpleirn Press showcases the best selections from our five annual creative contests in
fiction, nonfiction, drama, poetry, and art.

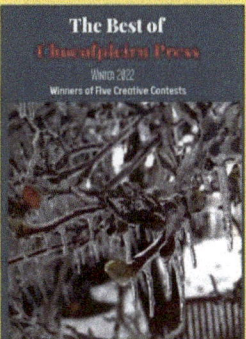

Choeofpleirn Press
www.choeofpleirnpress.com
choeofpleirnpress@gmail.com
A 501(c)(3) company

Printed in the USA
CPSIA information can be obtained
at www.ICGtesting.com
LVHW060905240923
759168LV00021B/896